Steel Barbs, Wild Waters

Steel Barbs, Wild Waters

Jerry Gibbs

Illustrated by
Joseph Fornelli

Published by Outdoor Life ® Books
SEDGEWOOD® PRESS, New York

Copyright © 1990 by Jerry Gibbs

Published by
   Outdoor Life® Books
   Sedgewood® Press
   750 Third Avenue
   New York, NY 10017

Distributed by Meredith Corporation, Des Moines, Iowa

Produced by Gracie Square Publishing Service
Book design by Jeff Fitschen
Typography by Trufont Typographers, Inc.

Gibbs, Jerry.
     Steel barbs, wild waters / Jerry Gibbs ; illustrated by Joseph Fornelli.
          p.   cm.
     ISBN 0-696-11006-7
     1. Fishing stories, American.   I. Title.
PS3557.I144S74   1990
813'.54 — dc20   90-060226
                                                            CIP

10   9   8   7   6   5   4   3   2   1

Printed in the United States of America

To the quiet heros,
pretty ladies, rascals and
other assorted characters
who are as much responsible
for this book as I am.
And to the fish.

Contents

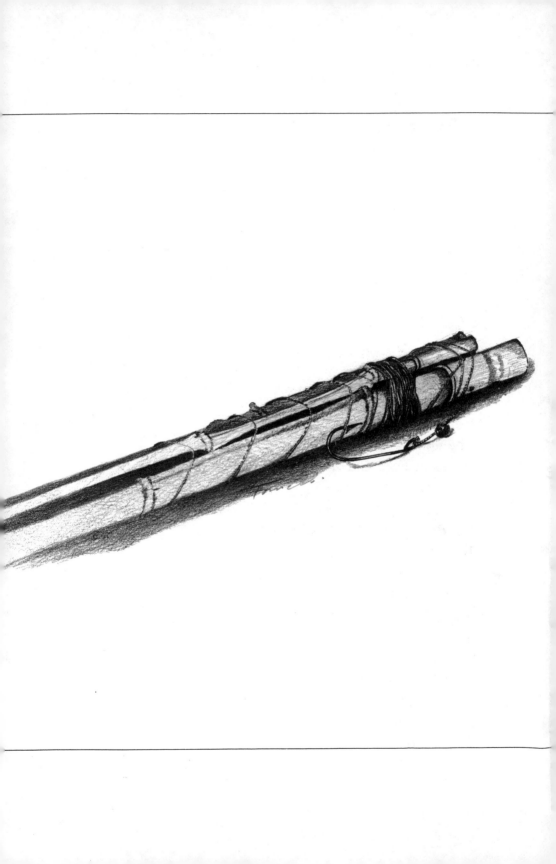

Preface

Many of these stories happened exactly as written. There are cases where several adventures involving the protagonists were combined in order that the events might live more strongly as a whole. Geography has been changed, none of the names used are real and certain events have been orchestrated or even fictionalized for the express purpose of making a better story or, as they say, to protect the innocent — and everybody else. In the end, the important thing is that the tales stand on their own, and that you enjoy reading them.

J.G.

Ironman

At 5:45 in the morning, Bill Selby's inner alarm woke him quietly and he lay on his back waiting for his head to clear. Before moving, he began a mental check, searching for weaknesses in the day's program. He could find no flaw in the plan formulated last night, the moves to each new area timed to accommodate the intricate crazy quilt of local tides. There were backups in case the wind changed. The fish would be there. They would get them. It was only a matter of size, of weight, to keep their lead.

Don't you wish, he thought, then rolled on his right side, swinging his legs to the floor and standing in one fluid movement. He reached up, stretching the stiffness from his arms, back and shoulders, feeling their soreness, the thickness of hands and arms from the previous two days of poling the skiff across thin water. Not too bad, though, he thought. Your wind's maybe not what it was, but you know the tricks now. He was sixty-three years old, had captained the largest blue-water craft and little inshore skiffs from the Canadian Maritimes to the Caribbean islands, and he was built like the trunk of a venerable oak.

In the pale light he looked with the usual wonder at his wife sleeping lightly, a wing of long blonde hair across her strong, high cheekbone, the fine ends moving slightly with her gentle breathing. Then he turned and padded in bare feet to the washroom.

He put water on the stove for coffee, returned to their bedroom to dress.

"Hello," Lynn said, sleepily. "How was your night?"

"I thought you'd sleep. I'm all right. Fine."

"How're your arms?" she rolled over, the sheet tracing the long, slim length of her. Last night she had kneaded and rubbed the muscles of his arms and shoulders, knotted and cramped from the poling, until they could relax.

"They're good. They'll be fine."

"It's going to be hot today."

"Mmm." It was her way of telling him to wear shorts. He rarely did, usually dressed in khakis whatever the heat, still not liking the fuss with sunscreen after all these years, unlike the young guides who lived, bathed in the stuff. Smart, too. Without it you paid. He put on a pair of faded tan shorts; the short-sleeved shirt was newer khaki. He went to start their breakfast.

It was the third day of the tournament, the big one in the world of flyrod tarpon events, and he had the lead; correction, Phil had the lead. Phil Anderson was the angler. He was guiding. It would be good to win. It kept you up there even though it shouldn't have to be necessary, even though you had, in a large part, been responsible for starting the game in the first place, had fished the big names, all of them, guided them while they carved the benchmarks of the sport. Wins helped in your backyard, too, helped remind all the young turks coming along now. In this business you never rested. He smiled. Or in most any other.

When they'd finished breakfast, and he knew it was time to go, he wished very much it was the next day or the one after. They gathered the dishes, and he went out to check the skiff.

He could have kept the boat in the water without trouble, but he never did, tournament or no tournament. He backed out the boat and saw Lynn leave in their car for the club.

They found Phil Anderson in the club dining room, sipping a coffee. He greeted them, smiling widely around his cup, long and lanky, shoving back a shock of sun-streaked, light-brown hair. Swinging his arm behind him, he put the cup on a window sill.

"God, I feel right today! You ready?"

"Going to do it today," Lynn said, too late to catch herself, knowing Billy hated that kind of thing. She took hold of his heavy upper arm a moment, holding it firmly. So many superstitions.

"Let's put her in," Billy said.

They launched the skiff on the old bumpy limestone ramp, and Phil brought the boat around front to the dock and tied up. The noise level had built slowly, and now it was a steady drone. They looked once again at the board on which the standings were written, confirmed their closest competitor, already knowing who it was, and suddenly it was time to go. Lynn kissed them both for luck. They dropped lightly into the skiff. Selby cranked the big engine, gentled the throttle forward, cupping the rim of the wheel, steering out the channel without having to think about it, big hard hands moving the tilt/trim control of the engine, dropping the trim labs. And then they leaped forward and were up on plane in seconds.

They left the main channel, cutting into a shallower staked pass that ran close to the first fat mangrove island.

They came to the first place. The sun was good, behind and to the right, so they could see well into the water, their shadows falling to one side of their intended direction. Billy killed the engine, raised it, and climbed onto the poling platform at the stern while Phil went to the forward casting platform. There he stripped off line, cast it, stripped it back, letting it drop in loose coils between his feet. In his left hand he held the fly, leader, the entire front taper and some of the belly of the line in wide loops that could be sent into the air with one rod stroke, the streamer then presented with one, maybe two false casts. Besides the necessary speed to lead and hit just ahead and slightly to one side of the moving fish, you could not afford the waving movement of a rod or fleeting shadow of aerialized line to fall across the tarpon's angle of vision. Those small suggestions of danger would send the huge creatures fleeing in terror like threatened bait from the shallow water.

Billy placed the foot of the forked pole firmly at the edge of the tiny channel that sliced into the bank they would work. Little puffs of gone-by blue-green algae billowed up like gray rotting leaves, stirred in solution. They skimmed across the channel, floated over the flat. He planted the pole, leaned a thigh against it and the skiff pirouetted to the right. They started down the flat in the thick silence of the wild place. High overhead a single man-o'-war bird wheeled and slid away across the sky.

For a little while there was no life on the flat, and they moved in silence that Phil was first to break.

"Ray coming," he said.

"Yep," Billy acknowledged. "See anything behind it?"

Phil stared into the little muds behind the feeding ray but saw no other fish that sometimes followed, picking up a free upturned meal in a ray's wake.

"Nothing."

"You see up ahead?" Billy asked.

"Funny water."

"Yeah. Let's take a look."

He doubled his efforts on the pole, pushing the skiff faster toward the bouncy surface just ahead, the disturbance often a tipoff to fish. You watched the surface as briefly as possible, trying to penetrate below it with your vision, down where the fish would show. Showed now.

"That's them," Phil said, low and tense.

The fish were moving right to left, dark blue-gray shadows, no real detail at this distance, except for size. They scanned the school, fast.

"Second fish's biggest, but all small fish," Billy said. "*Really* small. They're weight, though . . ."

It was nothing they did, but something unseen that suddenly spooked the school, bolting the fish ahead. Selby turned the boat right, back on course.

"Now you don't need to waste time on little stuff."

Phil grinned. They worked well as a team. "Good start, so quickly. Now we just need size. Keep 'em rolling, Billy."

"Just tryin' to please, boss," he said, inwardly wishing Anderson had not verbalized the business of a fast start. It was not a lucky thing.

They held on the bank, watching ahead against the possibility of more fish, bigger fish. They came to a small channel that snaked into the flat, the water light sapphire blue. Its edge dropped sharply, looking like a miniature western canyon wall with erosion-carved, distinctly stratified levels. They launched off the edge, floating across the deeper water as on air, motes of light sparkling ahead deeply in the clear water. The wall on the other side loomed up, climbing sharply, and they were on the bank again, the bottom rust colored, broken with beige and spots of brilliant jade. The surface was silk smooth, still, heaving gently. Then they saw the tarpon rolling.

There were many fish in the school. The backs and dorsals of five of them cleaved the surface, rolling slowly so you could clearly see the great scales covering their bodies. They were on a heading that required Selby to turn only slightly, then move ahead faster to close within casting range. Now they could see the forms of the fish below the surface, growing closer. Three more fish broke again, gracefully, moving calm and steady.

"God, they're happy," Billy said straining on the pole. "Get ready!"

"Lead fish . . ." Phil said.

"Yeah, now give it all you got."

The cast was away, line shooting out above the surface. It settled to the water, the streamer sinking, fluttering, then beginning its swim. The big lead fish moved its head, and the bulk of its body followed.

"She's turning, turning, keep it coming," Billy crooned low and steady. Then, "No, look at tha . . ."

With the lead fish still coming for the fly, a tarpon from back in the school bolted forward. They could see it clearly, mouth opening, engulfing the streamer, turning its head while Phil struck, jabbing hard three times to sink the barb. The lead fish was big, this one bigger. It had wanted the fly badly, and now its reaction to the hook was as violent as its attack. The fish went into the air short yards from the boat, gills rattling, open mouthed, the unhinged side-to-side head lashing that warns of what will follow. Still shaking, it crashed back, ripped along beneath the surface, the fine Dacron backing burning from the reel, then came up again, its entire length clearing the water. It was down now, ripping line through the surface on a totally reversed heading. Before the line had a chance to catch up, the fish again blew up, Phil trying somehow to give a moment of slack with each leap to keep the tippet from snapping. Selby pushed after it.

"Crazy. Crazy-as-hell fish," Billy said softly.

The tarpon made its first long run now, going straight away from them. As it ran it went through the surface once in a high, shuddering leap, slamming back and running again, always straight away. Selby cursed, poling hard. The run slowed and the fish began turning to the right. For the first time, Phil was able to spool line, then he realized the fish was circling. The tarpon came for them. Anderson put everything into reeling, then, in a rush, lost all he had gained as the fish completed its circle and started away once more.

Leaning hard on the pole, Billy tried to close the distance between boat and fish, Anderson not able to do anything now. The tarpon stayed under, sometimes boring left and right in short flurries, but always holding the same general heading out into the bay. After what seemed a very long time, the fish stalled. Billy slowly moved in, just a little, Phil reeling, pumping the heavy-butted rod, coils of wet backing piling up while his heart soared.

Though they were gaining line, Billy felt no confidence with this fish. Mainly, he did not like the way it ran always in one direction. The heading was away from the shallowest water where, with nowhere else to go, the fish would jump, and in jumping, tire itself. But for now the tarpon was coming.

The fish was close enough so the knot connecting the start of the backing with the end of the flyline was out of the water. The line was tight, knifing straight to the dark form of the fish clearly visible beneath the surface. Then Phil felt the thudding jerks.

"She's going to come up," he said.

It was the first time in a long while that the fish had tried to jump, and Billy wondered why it was doing so now. The flyline sliced the surface, rising above it, first the running section, then the taper, and then the bulk of the fish was in the air broadside to them. It lifted nearly straight from the water, huge etched scales vivid on its side, silver flanks gleaming in the sun, one bright, flat eye locked on them for a scant moment before the violent head-shaking began again.

The tarpon slammed back without grace, partly on its side, then with little apparent effort, plunged away ripping backing through the fingers of Phil's hand. He opened them instantly to keep the fine line from cutting his flesh, letting the drag of the direct-drive reel take over, the handle spinning so violently it was no longer distinctly visible. The fish ran straight away from them, taking all the recovered backing plus more. Billy put all his strength into the pole.

The fish bored ahead, and for a few moments they kept it from taking more line, then Phil turned his head slightly so Billy would be sure to hear.

"Line's getting low, and he's taking more," Phil said.

Billy was sweating hard, his breathing harsh. "Too deep now. I have to crank the engine."

He leaped from the mini tower, landing lightly despite his size, on the aft platform. He slammed the pole into its holders, lowered the engine, started it. They began motoring towards the fish just fast enough to allow Phil to pick up line. Billy had checked his watch when the tarpon took the fly. Now he looked at it again. They had been on for forty minutes, a time when many tarpon would begin coming steadily to the pressure of a rod. For awhile the water was too deep for poling, but they had closed the gap and now Billy killed the big engine and used the electric motors to position them while Phil tried to find some weakness in the fish. He began to turn the tarpon once with pressure on the right side, the side in which the streamer was embedded, but the fish straightened again, and all he could do was resist as strongly as he dared, keep the nagging worry of the pressure there and hope the fish would come to see that something as simple as letting its head turn and follow the unyielding pull would diminish that foolish annoyance. That was the beginning.

That was all you asked for at first. That one small act of acceptance by the fish was your opening, and you could not fail to act upon it. That was when you went to work in earnest, and you could never rest for a moment after that until it was over, one way or the other.

The lone hammerhead came from behind them and from the left so they did not see it until it passed the boat, cutting right and left, sensing the exciting tail and body beats of the troubled fish, trying to detect the blood odor that was not there and which, had it been, would arouse it further, hurry it in closing on its prey.

The tarpon was ahead, moving right, the shark still off to the left and closer. Billy turned on the electric motors. It was a big shark, and it looked dark brown in the water until it came closer to the surface, cut the surface with its dorsal, which was lighter, paler in the air.

In the bow, Phil cursed the shark softly.

The tarpon's position remained to the right, and Phil increased his pressure. The fish did not turn, but it slowed perceptibly. The skiff sliced ahead smoothly, quietly. The hammerhead circled out and Billy cut between it and the tarpon, so when the shark turned again he came for the skiff, sensed and probably saw it, and shot away. They saw it go, straight away, could see its riffling wake on the surface after its body was out of sight. But it did not stay away.

When the hammerhead returned, it did so from the right in a wide circle off the starboard quarter of the skiff. The tarpon was now on a heading that would take it across the bow, right to the left, when suddenly the presence of the shark or something else spooked it so it bolted on its heading, Phil letting line go with the rush.

"Better than close to Mr. Hammerhead," Phil said.

"Except that when the shark goes over there we won't see him, either."

"I know."

The electrics were on full now that the tarpon had run,

and Billy cut the skiff toward the hammerhead, which was tracking in the direction the tarpon had gone. This time he closed on it quickly. The shark was intent on the stressed signals of the tarpon, and though it was close to the surface, breaking at times, it had not seen the closing skiff. Billy left the electric motors, grabbed his pushpole and returned to the platform. At the last moment he turned the bow sharply to the left, paralleling the shark, then reared back on his feet and launched the pushpole like a javelin.

The pointed metal tip of the pushpole struck the shark on the back of the head — and bounced off. The hammerhead exploded, streaking off at right angles. This time it did not return.

"Nice." Phil said, waiting to see if the tarpon would continue holding.

Billy turned the boat, easing to where the pole floated.

"Shouldn't lose a fish to a shark that's under fifty feet away," Billy said. "If you can't throw the pole at him, you ought to be ready with something else. Maybe crank the big engine and run over him."

"It's a lot easier in shallower water, though," Phil said.

"Yeah, you're right. Better look to your fish."

The tarpon had stayed the distance he had run, and now Phil turned his concentration on forcing him back. Billy moved slowly to help him, the electrics humming low and steadily.

They had gone six miles out into the bay, two hours into the fight, before the tarpon acknowledged the unyielding pressure and began to come. It turned, and Phil led it on, pumping steadily, taking line, then following its swing past the skiff where he had to let it go again. Billy kept the angle of pressure against the fish where it would have the greatest effect, and in a little while Phil turned the tarpon again. Four times he turned the fish and four times led it nearer in the swing. And then, when they thought they would win, the fish would come no closer.

The tarpon stalled ten feet from the skiff. It held near the surface, plainly visible, blue and silver, the outlines of its fins and scales and eyes clear but abstractly mottled, in fluid motion from the water, from the moving water that broke the light. Each time he tried now, Phil turned and led the fish in its arc toward the skiff, and each time the distance closed to ten feet the tarpon resisted, swinging away. Billy tried to use the electrics to turn with the fish, trying to close ever-so-slightly on the swing, but the tarpon sensed it and made its turn more sharply away from them, maintaining its distance.

"I'm just going to have to wear it down," Phil said.

"Mean, stubborn sonofagun," Billy said.

He left the electrics and now took the gaff from its brackets. There had been no doubt from the beginning that if they could take the fish, they would. The tarpon was a weight fish, the fish they needed for the win, and so there could be no releasing the fish as there normally would be, and the gaff that Billy freed was the killer gaff. It shone silvery in the sunlight, eight feet long, the maximum length permitted by the tournament regulations. The bite of the hook was six inches, and the diameter of its metal was a full three-quarters of an inch. The point had been filed into three facets. The angles where each of the planes met were sharply formed for quick, cutting penetration.

"Try him again," Billy said. He walked forward, still along the gunwale, but close to the forward platform where Phil stood.

Phil brought the tarpon around again, and this time its swing seemed slightly closer, but it was still not enough. Twice they tried, gaining inches. Time became the enemy now. With each passing minute the hook of the streamer fly would cut a larger opening in the fish's mouth. With each effort to turn the fish, the strain on the tippet would further weaken the fine monofilament link and the knots that joined it to the other parts of the leader. Billy worked ahead of his angler on the platform.

"Back to the edge — as far back as you can," he said. He was on his knees in the bow of the skiff, the narrow outline of the bow perhaps less ominous to the tarpon.

The fish came around again, and Billy dropped flat, thrusting his feet and legs beneath the walkaround gunwales to hold himself against what would come, the tarpon swinging close, growing bigger, the guide beginning to reach. But the fish never closed enough.

The tarpon moved slowly forward, and with the pressure Phil would not relinquish, the bow of the skiff turned with the fish. The tarpon stalled, finning gently, unwilling to continue, to complete its arc.

"Turn him!" Billy demanded. "Right now, bring him around."

Phil held the rod almost parallel to the water, his grip high on the butt section of the rod blank, and slowly moved the fish. The tarpon turned, letting itself be led, swinging just close enough. Billy arched his upper body out over the water, reached and hit the fish in the middle of the back.

He jammed his legs, anchoring himself, holding the fish the way it was possible to do with even larger tarpon, but not this fish. Weary from the nagging, relentless pressure against it, but not broken, the tarpon erupted. It spun, and the gaff handle twisted in Billy's grasp, impossible to hold, impossible to release, Billy refusing to, feeling the grip of his legs fail, the skin on his chest and stomach and shins abrade as he was ripped over the bow. He felt his sunglasses on their monofilament snugger loop slapped from his face, pulled down around his neck as the fish dragged him underwater.

The rush dragged Billy twelve feet to the bottom. His feet and legs hit several times, once the ankle of his left leg slapping something hard and sharp, cutting. The speed of the fish's rush built an incredible crush of water against him. He tried to keep his eyes open, his vision blurred both by the water and buffeting speed through it. The run lasted for seventy-five feet. Then the tarpon slowed and stopped. Billy kicked his way to the surface, and he gasped for air. He turned on the fish, tried to pull himself toward it, lever the tarpon over with the handle. He heard Phil start to yell something from the skiff, and then he was pulled under again.

The fish ran toward the boat, then angled away another seventy-five feet before it stalled. Billy came to the surface again, coughing, sucking air into his lungs.

"Let go, let him go!" Phil yelled at him.

Billy pulled himself along the gaff handle, the fish looking huge as he reached it. He could see the fly still in the tarpon's mouth. Now he reached the end of the handle, grabbing the iron, the hook itself, at the bend where it entered the tarpon's back, and then the fish went down again.

The gaff handle slammed Billy in the side of the head but he held the hook, held with one hand. He was over the fish now, seeing it gray and blue in his half-blindness, terrifying in its strength and closeness. He held the hook, ignoring the screaming demand for air, worked his free hand forward, clawing, trying to lock on the fish's eye sockets, gills, mouth.

The fish ran for the boat, passed under it, the gaff handle slapping the bottom of the skiff followed by Billy's back, ramming hard once against the hull. On the other side of the boat the tarpon stopped. The gaff handle broke the surface,

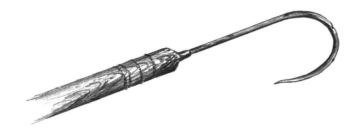

Billy still underwater with the fish, still fighting for a grip on it when Phil reached the gaff.

The tarpon spun, lashing against the locked gaff, Phil still lifting, bringing them in. Then the gaff's hook tore free, and the gaff circled back and up, the hook entering the lower part of Billy's right leg, going through the leg completely and cutting upwards through blood vessels and nerves. Billy came up on his back, his breath bursting in a terrible scream. In horror now, half out of the skiff, Phil worked to free the hook, then threw the gaff behind him. It clattered to the bottom of the boat.

Billowing clouds of blood colored the water. Phil caught the guide's uninjured leg, turned him, grabbed his arms, slid him over the low gunwale into the skiff. Billy lay on his back in the bottom of the boat, the long ragged wound pumping blood, and it was clear that major vessels had been severed and that they must do something very quickly. Phil scanned the interior of the skiff, began to open hatches while the flow of blood continued, spreading brilliantly on the deck. Billy's head was aft, the leg elevated slightly by the natural angle of the skiff.

"Ah, hell," he said, voice dry. He moved away the hand that was holding the wound, keeping tissue together. He hipped and elbowed himself onto the aft platform, yanked open a hatch and grabbed the rag he used to wipe oil. He rolled over again and tied the cloth around his leg above the wound as a tourniquet. Phil came back and grabbed the small bait net. He slipped its handle beneath the rag as a lever to tighten and release pressure of the rag tourniquet. There was another rag in the compartment and he tied it around the worst part of the wound. Blood pooled over the interior of the skiff but the flow was staunched, the wound oozing slightly, through and around the cloth.

Phil found cushions, putting them under Billy's head and neck. He slipped another atop a tacklebox, lifting the leg to rest, elevated. Then he raised the electric motors, dropped the main engine and started it. He moved the throttle forward. They were on plane in seconds.

"You doing OK?" Phil asked.

"Sure."

"You want something? Water?"

"Yeah, that'd be good. Here, I can rear up and steer a minute."

"No, I'll get it."

He slowed the boat, dropping them lower in the water, off plane, left the helm for the cooler, got the jug of water, cracking it open. Billy drank deeply.

"Just keep it there," Phil told him. He grabbed the wheel, straightened the boat and slammed the throttle forward as far as it went.

Billy watched the water as they ran. He held the net handle and from time to time turned it to loosen the rag and avoid cutting off blood flow completely to the leg. When he did that, the wound bled more freely, but not the way it had before. After tightening the tourniquet the fourth time, he tipped the water jug to his lips to drink again.

"God, I'm sorry," Phil said over the engine.

Billy lifted a big hand from the jug. "Nobody's fault. Something that happened." He let the hand drop. He leaned back, feeling tired, detached. The wound that had previously felt numb was now hurting, a throbbing hurt that came from deep within the leg and periodically sent stabs of searing pain up into his groin. He felt strangely outside himself, but his head was clear enough, and he began to think about how bad the wound might be and what it would ultimately do to him. He knew what it was going to do right now. It was tarpon season, he had been fully booked, and now he was out of it.

Maybe later in the year, he thought. There's a lot of good fishing later that almost everyone passes up. Should be in good shape again by then. Pick up a few fishermen you have to disappoint now. Disappoint, hell. Pick up a few bucks, too. You'll need it by then.

He was glad to see they were running in shallower water, passing the small mangrove islands, running light as though through air, getting closer, going home.

They were packed in at the club waiting for the boats, waiting for the weighing, and the air was electric, bristling with excitement. Some of the boats were coming in fast, small toys in the distance, growing very quickly into the powerful, exquisitely rigged machines they were as they neared. Lynn Selby stood outside the club with friends around her, feeling anxious, and then someone said there was Billy's boat coming, and she stood on her toes and saw that it was Billy's boat. She watched it carefully for a few moments, and knew something was wrong.

"It's Billy's boat," she said, "but Billy's not running it. Something must have happened."

"Oh, sure that's Billy," someone said.

"No. No, it's not," she told him, not turning away from the skiff.

They came in fast, Phil handling the skiff well, shutting down and reversing the engine hard to stop them quickly, and she saw Billy lying in the bottom of the skiff, the rag tourniquet around his leg and the awful brightness of the blood everywhere.

"My God," she said, Billy looking at her now, smiling tiredly, and she went down into the skiff to him.

"I'm all right, it'll be all right," Billy told her over her asking, Lynn looking from him to Phil, who was handling a line, now turning to her, everyone on the dock talking fast,

Phil trying to tell her but Billy's voice coming through over everything, the old, deep, rumbly voice, but not at all as strong as it normally was.

"Goddamned, gaff," Billy said. "Pulled out of a fish . . . got me."

"Oh, Billy," she said. She put her face to his. She looked at the leg, touched it gently. The crowd pressed in. Billy saw a ring of faces with little meaning to him. Phil was hollering for some help, and two big men pushed their way through. Both of them were guides. Carefully, they lifted Billy's bulk, moved him from the boat onto the dock, back into shade. He did not like it at all on his back, looking up at the standing crowd. In a short while he heard the ambulance siren rising, falling, growing closer, louder.

They had him on the stretcher quickly despite his size, and the crowd was pushed back, friends helping move the rubbernecking strangers. They went quickly down the dock. The one boat in the tournament they had worried about was coming in, its fish laid out silver and flat in the cockpit, broad tail curled up touching the edge of the aft platform, massive scales sharply outlined in the late afternoon sun. It was a good fish, probably enough to give them the win. Billy looked at the tarpon closely as they moved on. Good fish, for sure. But not nearly as large as the one he and Phil had fought. Not even close.

Later, in his hospital room, Lynn told him about the seventy-eight stitches, the nerves and the vessels patched, and some worry about his walking, which would be easy to believe given the way the leg pounded now like a world-class hangover. Then she began really putting her mouth on the fish. He watched her, looking lovely in her anger, working over the fish's lineage many generations past, its present character and ultimate reward, far better than any of his oldest cronies would have been able to do. He started laughing softly.

"You think it's funny!" she exploded.

"No. You. You've got a mouth. Some mouth." He shook his head incredulously.

She leaned on him, buried her face against his for a moment, then stood up, quickly brushing away a suspicion of tears.

"You're going to be fine."

"Sure," he told her. "It's not the fish's fault. Fish does what it's supposed to do. Even friend shark. Sharks got to eat, too. That's what they're there for. To clean up."

He was somewhat groggy, as though he'd slipped down a few extra rum runners too quickly after being in the heat all day. "Tarpon are in there, in the shallows trying to keep themselves going, keep their species going, fat and happy and sexy, and we're the ones who bust in on them." He found it hard to concentrate. "That's what *we're* for," he continued, "just like any other predator. That's what we'll keep doing. That's what I'll keep doing."

"You get yourself healed first."

"Sure. This one won't get me. Don't you worry." He held her shoulder with one big calloused hand.

"I won't," she said.

Then he began drifting off, seeing the bright, color-changing water and the line of creature-shaped clouds curling crazily on the horizon, the sun bright overhead, very good for seeing fish. Then he was asleep.

(Author's note: In recent seasons there has been a distinct trend toward on-the-water release in tarpon tournaments.)

The Shanty

The ice was dead gray. It stretched as far as you could see looking north up the big, ragged lake. Snow that once brightened the expansive frozen surface had long since melted into hills of slush or two-inch-deep sheets of frigid water that the wind riffled passing through. Beneath the thin layers of water, the ice showed gray and bleak. It was still safe, though, still over a foot thick, and far from turning the almost black that would herald its final rottenness.

At the access parking lot stood remnants of a once-bustling ice-fishing village, shanties that had been pulled hastily from the melting lake to avoid being frozen in, locked solid when the weather turned again in the night. The shanties stood in disarray around the perimeter of the access, some

slanted in final salute at acute angles toward the lake. Some
had lost their roofs, and one was completely over on its side.
The very few remaining ice houses on the lake were those
owned by the dedicated, the hard-core regulars who would
fish in them daily, sometimes in the nights, keeping close
watch on what the weather did. Everyone else who continued to fish the ice would do so on the good days, bringing
their equipment out and back on sleds or in packs when each
outing ended.

In the North Country it was the worst time of year.
Roads crumbled or turned to sheets of mud. Melting snows
revealed the mounds and clots of preserved winter litter.
Trees stood exhausted and bare, their buds yet to color. But
sap was beginning to run in the sugar bush, and the crows
had returned, their sharp tenor rasping with the bonging of
ravens across the woodland valleys. You could say it was
spring. The way it is spring in the North.

The two men and the big, black Labrador retriever were
about fifty yards out of the access, heading south across the
ice toward a long point that thrust from shore, guarding the
entrance to the bay. Their boots set up a rhythmic swishing
in the places where the sheets of shallow water covered the
ice. The dog ran ahead exploring, quartering, coming back to
check on the men. Its owner, Bud Tuttle, was pulling the sled
with its boxed-in sides that carried most of their equipment.
The dog was very happy.

"I ought to harness all your energy, foolish dog," Tuttle
told the Lab. "This sled is getting waterlogged and damned
heavy."

"Here, let me haul it for awhile," said the other man. He
was a little shorter, but broader, stockier than Tuttle. His
name was Earl Waite. He was Tuttle's old friend and the two
had not seen one another for some time.

"Nah, you're a guest today," Bud told him. "I only let my
guests haul the sled on the way back with a load of fish when
I'm beat from digging holes."

Earl laughed. "That's all right," he said.

The dog was exploring the corners of a shanty they passed. "Ace, get over here," Tuttle called. The dog completed its territorial marking and trotted obediently back.

Far off the point were several ice fishermen. Some had set out tip-ups but most were working short jig rods or jigging sticks for yellow perch. Around the point and not far from it was a fragile ice shanty of wood framing and black tarpaper.

"I don't know why they still fish out that far," Bud said. "Those big schools of yellows are moving in here by now. If they want some deep water, they can find it at the point."

"That drops off pretty fast, if I remember right," Waite said.

"You bet. Then it shallows up soon as you start getting into the mouth of the bay. Look at that shack. That's old Rene Tatro's. He moves it once all winter, from out off the point, back to where he is now. He's in there most all the time, day or night. If anybody catches fish through a hole in the ice, it's him."

They sloshed on a little way without talking.

"Course they'll have better chance of nailing a passing trout or salmon farther out there, but I pick up trout right at the drop, too, where we'll fish. Anyway, perch is what you want, I think."

"I haven't had a good perch feed in so long . . . almost forgot how they taste," Earl Waite said.

"We ought to start on the near side of the point, then just work around the other side of it near the drop until we find them. That church steeple and white boat house are lined up right on the drop," Bud pointed.

The slush was melted into clear water over the ice at the point's near side where they stopped the sled. Earl grabbed the auger first. "Where you want to start?" he asked.

"Oh, just about there," Tuttle pointed. "Try another out just a little, going toward the point. I'll stick your jig rod and box right here. Some mousies are in the cup."

He placed the little styrofoam cup holding the live maggot bait beside the box and dragged the sled through the wet going a little toward the point. The dog splashed water, bounding like a spring colt.

The first hole finished, Earl walked over and the two men grabbed the auger, alternating grips along the handle to cut the second hole fast. The ice drill was extremely sharp. It cut with a grating sound, piling up white ice shavings around the forming hole as it sank. Just before breaking through to water it stalled; they backed it once, then gave it a hard forward movement, and the drill went on through. They pulled it up and water gushed around the hole for a moment. Bud went to the sled and removed the sieve, dipping out ice chips, clearing the hole. Then he went to the first hole and did the same.

Earl freed the hookless attractor spoon and the little ice flies secured to the jig rod guides. He baited half a mousie on each fly, then sent the silver spoon first, followed by the flies on droppers above it, down into the hole. He found bottom and cranked the baitcasting reel a few turns to work the rig just a couple of feet up.

"That's the trick," Bud said. "Work from the bottom on up. You never know where you'll hit them. Except I'll be a little deeper and I don't think they'll be flat on bottom."

"You using the same rig?"

"Except for the spoon," Tuttle said. "I put on one of those Rapala jigging plugs. You know, the kind that swim around in little circles when you move them up and down. Never can tell when a stray trout might like to eat. Or a pike." He walked back to the second hole.

It was quiet across the lake. A slight breeze came from the western shore, and with it the floating strains of song sung in a dry, crackly voice.

"Who's doing the singing?" Waite called over.

"That'll be old Rene in the shack."

"Entertainment on the ice!"

Bud laughed. "Rene spends a lot of hours alone in there. Cooks some of the fish he catches right on his heating stove. Keeps a bottle of rum for company. If he gets really tuned we'll have some music."

The first holes produced nothing. After a time Bud called over.

"Let's move 'em," he said. "We ought to go around just off the point. Why don't you try farther out, and I'll go in more."

Earl nodded, reeling up his rig. He walked in an arc, paralleling Tuttle. Bud was already drilling at his spot. When he finished, he started toward Earl, who met him halfway.

"That's probably good on this angle," Bud said. "Just about dead off the point."

"But out some."

"I think so."

Strains of a song in Quebec French came across to them from the shanty. They turned toward the little shack. Bud smiled.

"He hasn't really got started. You'll see. He switches back to English sometimes."

The dog appeared around the corner of the musical shanty, snuffling at the edges.

"Ace, get over here," Tuttle yelled. The Lab started toward them.

They dug the new hole for Earl, and when the water gushed through, it was lighter, a gray-blue.

"We're deeper, all right," Waite said.

"Maybe too deep. Well, try a little."

Ace came up panting, nuzzled Tuttle's leg and explored the new hole.

"Good boy," Bud praised him, rubbing ears hard. "You leave the old man's shack alone, hear?" Then he straightened and spoke to Earl. "Old Tatro's got some fishing system in there. He doesn't just fish a couple holes. Got a whole long trench he keeps open, a bunch of fishing lines spaced along over it on a rack. The lines come off little wood spools up through open brackets on the rack and down into that trench. He's got the brackets lined with plastic so the line won't fray going through. Fish hits, he just plucks the line from the bracket, hand-over-hands it in — unless it's a big one. If it is, he can let it run off the spool. Thought of everything, I guess. Slick as owl dung in the rain. Only thing I've seen up to it is those commercial fishing houses up to the St. Lawrence where they fish Tommy cod and you rent a place inside with your lines, kind of like a saltwater party boat, only it's through the ice."

Earl shook his head, fascinated. "Sounds like a production line."

"Sometimes he catches fish likc it was. Old geezer. I worry one day he'll slip through that trench, though, if he gets enough booze in him."

"Go catch a fish," Earl said. "We're hurting for dinner."

"I know it."

The dog trotted ahead of Tuttle going back to the sled. Earl watched them go, counting off line in two-foot pulls to the bottom. It's deep, he said to himself. He cranked his reel, counting, until he figured he was fishing at fifteen feet. Then he looked back toward the point, past his friend and the dog, past old Rene's ice house to the big bay, and wondered if they would end up fishing there. Overhead, streaks of thin clouds backed by a high, gray dome, gave the sky the look of cool, polished tombstone. The sky had distinct limits this day, and when he looked as far north as he could, the lake seemed a very lonely place to be, and he was glad he had company.

His second hole produced nothing, and when he decided more time would not help, Earl started in. Tuttle had done no better. With the sled, Ace in the lead, they headed around the far side, the bay side of the point, closer to the old man's shanty. Earl could see that the black and gray shack was leaning toward the left. Bud saw his friend examining the ice house.

"Wind and snow, probably," he said. "He builds it up new every year. It's not the strongest thing. I guess we'd better fish here awhile."

They drilled their holes inside the edge of the dropoff where the bottom rose quickly from 40 to 18 feet, then gently shallowed to the curving beach. This time they drilled their holes closer together, more for company than any insight into fish location.

Rene's ice shanty had been quiet for some time. Suddenly, the disembodied voice boomed strongly across the ice. The song, sung in English this time, was something about Texas ladies, and sunshine and babies, and the old man sang it high in his nose in grand country fashion. For the time and place, the song was delightfully incongruous. Then Earl felt the peck through the short, stiff jigging rod, and he struck with a quick, short snap.

"Hey," Bud said. "About time."

Earl did not crank the fish in. He used the tip of the jig rod, and his non-rod hand in a kind of alternating cat's-cradle, to pick up line and bring the small fish in. He dumped the monofilament on the ice, the yellow perch following.

"Nice," he said. "Nice perch."

The fish was fat with spawn, gleaming golden brassy, its black vertical barring vivid. Instinctively, it splayed its gill covers with their sharp end points, and arched its spiny dorsal. Earl brought it to the sled, placed it in the tall white plastic bucket, and returned to the hole. The loops of stiff mono on the ice would soften quickly in the water and the spoon and little flies drop back to precisely the same level where the first fish had hit.

Hearing the elevated tone of their voices, the black Lab came trotting back from one of his exploratory circuits. He came up just as Bud hit a fish.

"They're just a couple feet off the bottom," Bud said happily.

"That's where mine hit."

The dog danced around Tuttle's hole, leaped for the perch as it hit the ice.

"Ace, back!" Tuttle ordered. The dog stepped back reluctantly, wanting the fish, snuffing at it. "You'll get fin-pricked, you mutt," Tuttle grumbled affectionately. "Not to mention slobbering up my dinner."

They took two more fish each, but it was not fast and they spread out, drilling new holes in the same area, looking for the main school that had to be nearby. They went shallower, still picking up fish, drilling a line of holes toward the bay, then moving out on the drop again. That's where they hit the school.

The fish were tightly concentrated, so that holes a couple of yards apart meant the difference between occasional fish, or rapid action. They ended with four holes drilled in a tight cluster, alternating fishing them as one cooled and another became productive.

In his shack the old-timer began another country-western song. You could not hear clearly all the words of the verse, but each time he reached the invitational chorus he boomed.

"Let's chase each other 'round the room tonight," the old man sang, his Quebecois English highlighting unexpected places, sounding nice.

"He's getting there," Bud laughed.

"So are we," Earl said, sticking another fish.

"Let's string out these holes and connect them," Bud said. "We can keep moving right on top of them, just like old Rene's trench."

They dropped the jig rods and augered new holes connecting the old ones. Then Tuttle grabbed the long steel ice spud from his sled and widened the slot. The opening was a long, rough rectangle. They worked it together, moving with the fish.

Ace stayed with them now, darting happily, feinting at each new fish. Over at the shanty, Rene was singing in

French, a sad-sweet, melodious ballad. Two big crows circled over the bay.

Just then Bud struck, and this time the little jigging rod's tip went down, line tearing from the reel with a soft zipping sound.

"No perch!" Earl yelled. He reeled his own line in quickly.

"For sure, no perch," Bud said. The fish had finished its initial run and Tuttle was getting line now, reeling smoothly. Then the fish went again. This run was shorter but deeper, and when the fish was turned it came only a little way before going a third time, this run toward the point and close beneath the ice. Bud thrust his rod tip into the trench.

"He's awfully close to the top. He'll cut me off on the edges if I'm not careful."

The dog heard the excitement in the men's voices and came close, watching, tail wagging merrily.

"I got him coming," Bud said. He reeled faster now, gaining line.

"Trout! Nice rainbow," Tuttle said.

Earl raced for the sled. "You got a net? A gaff or something . . ."

"Hell, no." The fish was at the surface. It thrashed, showering Tuttle on his knees, reaching for it. Then the fish ran again, forcing the angler to punch the rod tip into the trench.

"I got heavy line," Bud said. "If I can get him to hold on top a second I can scoop him with one hand and just swing him over."

The fish tired and came to the pull. It lay on the surface, Bud holding it with the half-raised rod, reaching under its belly with his left hand, then coming back all the way with the rod overhead, the fish arcing brightly through the air to the ice, gleaming there, bold magenta stripe on its side. The big rainbow arched its body, hard muscles lifting it from the ice. Earl grabbed it, feeling it slip away instantly. The fish spun on the ice, flopped, and Ace was on it, but not fast

enough. Its last powerful effort took the rainbow from between the dog's feet back into the trench, the Lab seeing it all,
following it, hitting the frigid water after it.

"Ace, back!" Tuttle shouted.

Knowing about injured waterfowl, the black dog
scanned the surface for a moment, then ducked under.

"Ace!" Tuttle bellowed. He pounded with his boot heel
on the ice.

Earl jabbed his jig rod under, searching futilely.

Tuttle ran to the sled, came back with the ice sieve and
dropped to his belly. He jabbed the wide scoop into the water
followed by his arm to the shoulder, searching frantically for
the dog. The water went through his down jacket, painfully
cold.

"Ace, Ace!" he called. "Oh, the damned, stupid . . ."

Earl searched frantically for some way to help.

"I can't hold onto this scoop," Bud said, rolling onto his
knees, his hand now gone angry red.

"Here, give it to me," Earl grabbed the sieve. He was
down and scooping on the other side of the wide trench.

A scream sliced the air. They saw Rene's shanty rock
once before one tarpaper wall exploded, splintering flimsy
framing, spewing the old man in green suspenders and baggy
wool trousers. His white hair flared in ragged streamers, his
eyes rolled madly, and from his sunken cavern-dark mouth
came a wavering tortured wail. Rene Tuttle hit the ice running. He slipped to all fours in the water covering the ice,
gained his feet and churned for the shore of the point, not

seeing the anglers, not seeing anything now, but the safety of shore.

"The beast!" he screamed. "The beast, the beast!"

When he reached the shore he crashed into the woods.

The two anglers were up now, heading for the destroyed ice house, running wordlessly. They reached the shattered shanty and stared in. Inside was total shambles. Tackle was strewn in every corner. A half-filled two-quart can of kernel corn lay scattered like confetti. Bits and pieces of his lunch joined the yellow niblets. An empty rum bottle lay on its side in the debris. And in the middle of it all was Ace, tail beating a wet tattoo as he wolfed down old Rene's food and lapped up the corn.

"Ace you fool!" Tuttle said. "Come here." The dog even gave up eating to come. Bud grabbed him around the shoulders and the Lab shook his hind quarters, showering both of them.

"I can't believe this," Earl said.

"It's real, all right. Look at that setup. Ace must have boiled right up in the middle of that trench looking like the devil himself."

They both began laughing. They sat in the debris and could not contain the relief.

"The poor old geezer probably thought it was old Ned — or the lake monster we're supposed to have," Bud said wiping tears from his face.

"Oh yeah, I remember, like the one in Loch Ness," Earl said.

"Ace, you are a monster all right. Nothing's hurt with the fishing setup anyway," Bud pointed. "But the shack's sure finished."

"I'm shutting down the stove," Earl said.

Ace squirmed to get back at the food.

"No more, you. You've done enough for the day," Bud told the dog. "I'm going to call poor Rene. He won't believe me. Maybe I shouldn't tell him the truth. I bet he goes on the wagon from this. I've got to fix his shack for him. Maybe when he calms down, he'll help me get it off the lake. God, I wonder if I can ever get him back on the ice again."

"We better get out of here before we start freezing," Earl said. "I'm starting to feel it."

"So am I. I think my arm's frozen."

They staggered back to the sled, piled up equipment and headed back toward the access, walking fast.

They looked at one another and started again, laughing so hard walking became difficult. The dog ran from one to the other, pleased with it all. Finally Earl forced himself to quiet.

"You know," he said, "along with everything we have enough fish for supper."

"Good thing," Bud told him. "Nobody'll believe the rest."

Overhead, along the shoreline, two crows headed north in silence into spring.

Wings of Fear,
Claws of Terror

There were two things in life that terrified Mary Hollister. Not the things you would expect to frighten a sophisticated, cosmopolitan woman — the darkly hovering threat of nuclear disaster, for instance, or the likelihood of a new Love Canal popping up in her own neighborhood. Not at all. Mary Hollister feared bears and bush planes above everything else. She was also married to a fisherman.

To be fair, bears were a childhood fright. Big, padding brownies; grizzlies with horrible comealong claws, always inescapable in the deadly slowness of nightmare running. Bears seemingly faded with childhood. Then came aircraft. She quickly learned that flying, even in large, scheduled aircraft, was not something she liked at all. The thought of small planes was absolutely chilling. Then she married Steve, and inevitably there came Alaska slowly emerging like an artichoke heart with each tantalizing peel of leaf. Alaska — the fisherman's paradise. For her, Alaska meant bears. And little planes.

A few of the pilots who flew these little planes visited their home. She also heard stories from Steve's cronies who had fished the great land and elsewhere in the north, having been transported there by aircraft of minuscule proportions. She studied their bush pilot guests in fascinated horror, thinking of them as otherworldly creatures. She filed each new tale in a private arsenal of determination. It was to be her ammunition of refusal when Steve would finally ask her to go. Tonight was the clincher, the seal upon her decision if one had ever been needed.

It was a fine party. That was a fact, even though she and Steve had orchestrated the thing. The grilled steelhead were succulent under the soy, dark sugar and rum barbecue sauce. Pepe the miniature mongrel had not bitten anyone and was happily at work retrieving bullfrogs down at the river. While moving between deck and kitchen to ensure the flow of assorted delicacies, she heard several wondrously terrifying new stories. After tonight, no one, not even Steve, would be able to change her mind.

Always, everyone in the stories escaped the flipped plane or fallen helicopter by getting out fast — before the craft caught fire — or there would not have been the stories. She listened incredulously as someone told about the rescue plane, too heavily loaded with crash survivors to lift off the small lake. One man volunteered to stay behind. He fastened a rope to a strut or something on the float plane, the rope stretched ashore and tied to a stout tree. The pilot increased the engine rpm's steadily higher until the little single engine craft strained and trembled, a furious chained beast, while the water curled, hollowed and blew away in the prop wash.

And then the volunteer stepped in, swinging his ax in a neat semicircle, going up on his toes, coming down smartly with the blade to sever the rope. The plane shot off and up as though released by an aircraft carrier catapult. The pilot came back for the volunteer later.

On her way to supervise the dessert, Mary heard the episode from James Bay. The little plane carrying its load of sports circled the tiny camp airstrip after dark. The runway lights — the headlights of trucks and Jeeps parked around the strip's perimeter — shown brightly. The only thing was, the Indians who ran the operation chose that evening to demonstrate displeasure over some recent slight or possibly long-range governmental policy. The landing area they were illuminating was in fact a mud tidal flat rather then bulldozed strip. And as the plane made its approach they switched off the lights. The pilot's steel-trap reflexes saved the party in a spectacular fly-by. Eventually the disgruntled natives led the plane back to safety. Rattled from the experience, the pilot seduced the camp cook into flying off with him the next day. The pair disappeared late the following afternoon, and reappeared a day later crashing into a private yacht marina back in civilized country. They said the pilot had been drinking. Neither he nor the cook suffered bodily injury. A special plane had to be sent to get the sportsmen out of the camp.

It was when the lemon chiffon dessert was being served that Mary felt real stomach pangs. Hank Jameson — the wildlife photographer — was giving a graphic account of trying to obtain some grizzly bear aerials with a zealous young turk of a pilot. Jameson and his wife, Jill, had to coax the flyboy to work. He was deep into the current edition of one of his favorite comic books. They found the bears. The big bruins were clawing salmon from the river. The light was wonderful. Jill loaded camera bodies, snapped on the right lenses while the young pilot sent the Beaver in a Kamakazi dive, tipping the single-engine on its wings and holding it there to pirouette in tight circles.

"Did you get it, did you get the shot?" the hotshot yelled over the roar of the De Haviland engine.

The bulkheads vibrated. Small, unfastened items danced about the plane, and Jill turned a bilious green.

"How in hell can I get the shot," said Jameson. "The centrifugal force is so bad I can't pull my camera arm off the overhead!"

They finally managed to fire off several rolls with the motordrive while the pilot did fly-bys, the photography door and window nearly parallel to the ground, the couple held fast by their seatbelts.

To her everlasting credit, Jill did not become sick until after they landed and were staggering away from the plane.

"Only thing I could think of later," Hank told his audience, "was the game my kid told me they sometimes play in his dorm. See, they get this three-foot length of PVC pipe, sit it on its end in the hallway. Then you have to put one eye to the tube and run around it ten times. Then you look up fast and try to run down the hallway. Guess they just bounce off the walls like a ball in a racket court. Evidently knocks hell out of your equilibrium."

T wo months later Mary Hollister was not at all sure how it happened that she was standing at the airport in King Salmon, Alaska, fresh off the flight from Anchorage.

"How was it for you?" Steve asked, concerned.

"Really, it wasn't too bad. It was *smooth*, you know. And the wine was lovely."

"Good," he told her. "Now I've got to find our man from the camp."

He left her with the luggage. It was early July — just the start of the sockeye run — and because of that, Steven had promised, the bears would not be eating salmon yet, and they would be lucky to see one. But she was worried about them anyway. She also worried about getting to camp. It was going to be just a little bit smaller plane, Steven had said; and she envisioned something not much smaller than the aircraft she had just disembarked. After all, the military was landing big jets nearby, weren't they? And here was Steve back now with this big fellow smiling so nicely at her.

"Mary, this is Pete Marks," Steve said. "He's our bush pilot."

"*Bush* pilot!" she exclaimed!

Then everything started happening too fast. They hurried out the door, loaded into a station wagon and drove off. In a moment, they passed some hangers. She noted the small planes and looked for the medium-sized one they would take.

Pete was talking to her, calm and friendly, his slow, deep voice just giving you confidence, and she had to answer him about the trip and how much — how little — fishing she really did. The car stopped and he helped her out, taking her emergency travel bag, opening the back of the wagon for their luggage. She turned and stared.

"What's that?" she demanded.

"Oh. I guess that's ours," Steve said somewhat doubtful.

"I'm not going," Mary told them.

"Mary, there was a problem . . ."

"No. No problem. I'll just go back later today on the commercial flight. I don't want to spoil your trip. No problem."

"We were to have a twin engine," Pete told her. "Just a little, uh, maintenance needed doing. This fine old Beaver is probably the safest single that flies, Mary. Let me show you something."

He guided her by the arm to the little plane and she could feel the palms of her hands cold and damp. Steve took out the bags and carried them to the plane.

Marks was good. He could have gentled wild horses. He

rumbled on, moving easily, pointing out everything, an old-time family doctor who still made house calls.

"And we'll be going slow and not very high, and there's just a bunch of swell places we could sit right down on at any time. Why those big floats are just like air cushions, and the whole thing is just about as safe as sitting home in your favorite curl-up chair with the cat," he told her.

I could keep my eyes tight and pray us all the way, she thought.

"You can sit right up front and keep an eye on me instead of being all scrunched up in back. Let *him* sit on the bags."

They were three-quarters of the way through the flight when she looked somewhere other than straight out of the sky. She dared to glance at the ground or the water passing below. It was like being stuck at the top of the Ferris wheel at a carnival. She looked away quickly and continued to hold on to her seat.

She was strapped in and Pete was going around to the pilot's door when she whispered dryly to Steve in back of her, only slightly turning her head.

"I knew I shouldn't have come," she whispered. "Why are you letting this happen to me? You know we surely will be killed, Steven."

Then Pete started the engine.

They landed smoothly, in Katami National Park, near the Brooks River where they were to fish, though she knew there was no way she could fish at all, perhaps not even stand. They taxied around smoothly, then Pete killed the engine and came around to help her out, she apologizing for the coldness of her hand, finding it was indeed possible to stand, though she felt a nerve twitching in her right leg.

"We'll see you folks later," Pete said suddenly.

"You're *going*!" Mary asked, disbelieving, knowing they would never get out.

"Gotta make a living," Pete said. "You did just fine flying, you know. I get some much worse than you."

They watched the Cessna taxi out, and then there was the lady warden or park cop or whatever she was standing in front of them neat and trim in her tailored uniform.

"Welcome to Katami National Park and Reserve, and the Brooks River," said the lady ranger. "The salmon run is early this year. It's in full swing. Please empty your pockets of any candy bars, granola, gum, or other snacks. Our bears are thick, as you might expect. And when you walk, keep out of the tall grass."

Mary grabbed Steve's arm to keep from dropping.

The glass of water helped. She was still dazed, still functioning like a robot, while Steve assembled his tackle quickly.

"Are you going to come?" he asked her.

"Of course I'll come. If you're going to be eaten by a bear, it might as well take both of us together. Besides, I'm not going to stay here alone."

Steve was in waders; she had on rubber knee boots. They started toward the river on the well-used path that went out, then cut down right into the tall grass.

Whether it's Bror von Blixen's or Capstick's Africa, they call it *long* grass, Mary considered. Now in Alaska, it's *tall* grass. She walked quickly to keep pace with Steve. It doesn't matter, tall or long, it's where you're not to go because you can't *see*, for Godsake, what might be a couple of yards anywhere around you! And why was Steve in such a rush to get eaten, that he was almost running?!

"Why are you going so *fast*?" she demanded.

"Want to fish."

The tall grass went down fairly close to the river and then they broke out. The river flowed steady and riffly, a nice looking stretch ahead of them, then a little way below it made a sharp bend and disappeared behind the tall grass. There would probably be a deep, washed hole around that bend. Across the river was a hill climbing sharply from the shore.

"See, no problem from the tall grass," Steve said. "Look how beautiful." He shook out line, saw his leader was cut back almost to the butt section, but didn't waste the time tying on a new one. He dug out a bright streamer, and had to bend the hook eye open slightly to get the heavy monofilament section through.

"What a country," he said. "See, no bears. Look, there's a couple more fishermen down there." He pointed down toward the bend where two anglers worked their flies. "Isn't that pretty, there's a horse up on the slope across the river." Then he waded into the river.

Mary stood somewhat back from the water on what had been river bed in higher water, hugged her arms around her and inspected her surroundings. She looked at the two anglers down river, then across the river up the slope at the horse. Steve was already casting, letting the fly swing downstream.

"Steve," she called loud enough so he could hear over the water.

"Yeah?"

"You better look again."

"What?"

"At the horse."

"Why?"

"It's a bear."

Steve jerked attention from his fly and looked up the slope. He looked very carefully.

"You're right. It is a bear. But it's just sitting there watching us. We'll keep a good eye on him."

She said nothing.

Downriver the other anglers may or may not have seen the bear. They were wading across the river now, above the bend, probably seeing a better drift on the far side. It was not that deep but the water came to just below the wader tops of the shorter angler.

"Ho!" Steve shouted. "Fish. Oh, yes . . ."

A medium-size salmon skated across the surface, disappeared to run down, then back upstream. Mary watched the fish jump and turn the river splashy. The fish started down again. Watching it she also saw that the anglers downstream had moved around the bend. The taller angler's head was just visible above the tall grass. The short fisherman was out of sight. Mary looked back at Steve and his fish again, then froze in horror for one second.

"Steve!" She screamed it. "The bear! The bear is coming!"

Thigh-deep in the river, Steve pivoted, saw the big light-brown shape moving down, covering distance in that ripply fluid way they move. Steve bore down hard on the fish, trying to break it off.

She heard the shouts down river, saw an arm now, as well as the head, of the taller angler. They must have heard her scream, or seen for themselves what was happening. And then she saw the head of the shorter angler appearing, disappearing, then reappearing like a jack-in-the-box as the man jumped behind the tall grass to gain a view of the descending bear. It was something from a situation comedy, except that it was real.

"Do something, Steve!" she yelled. "We've got to get out of here or we'll be eaten!"

"I am!" He was yanking now on his fly line, but the heavy leader section would not break. The sockeye that had triggered the bear was thrashing in the shallows on the far bank downstream.

Mary saw the other anglers coming around the bend again, heading for the shallow spot where they had waded across. She saw them stop suddenly, spin around and run off. Then she saw that the bear had nearly reached the river. It was heading directly for Steve's fish.

"Oh I knew we shouldn't have come," Mary wailed. Steve dropped his rod, yanked on the line with both arms, but nothing broke and the hook would not bend or pull out.

She ran up the bank nearly to where the tall grass started.

"Leave it, Steve! Leave the rod and run!" she screamed.

From her elevated spot she saw the downriver anglers struggling across the river in the deeper water, trying frantically for the near shore. The tall man was up to his wader tops in the current and he had the short man skimming along on his back in a kind of lifeguard neck carry, and the short fisherman was yelling at his friend, "Higher! Higher! Higher!" Mary could hear it very clearly. And now, Steve or no Steve, she was going to run.

Steve chewed madly at his flyline which parted neatly, and the bear was on the fish, looking enormous, and finally here came Steve.

At the edge of the tall grass she watched Steve run, the severed flyline streaming from the rod guides. She watched in awe at what the bear had done to the salmon, snapping it in half with a bite, then finishing it off completely with two more.

"Let's go!" Steve shouted.

Before she turned down the path, Mary saw the bear was unhurriedly pushing across the river directly for them.

"I know he's going to eat us, Steve!"

"Get going!" he shouted. "Run!"

"You're not *supposed* to run."

"To hell with that, run!"

They ran up the path in the tall grass, gaining elevation nearer the lodge, seeing behind the swaying grass where the bear followed. They reached the clearing and they could see the bear below advancing slowly now, unsure with the human commotion from above. And then they were at the lodge. When they looked down again, they could see nothing but the grass.

"Where'd he go?" someone said.

They turned to see the taller of the two anglers who had fled the river ahead of them. The short one was standing a little behind, his face ashen.

"He's gone now," Steve said, panting. "He followed us nearly all the way back."

Mary leaned against the railing of the deck unable to talk.

"I guess he figured I had more fish," Steve said.

"Sure," the tall fisherman said. "Thought you were a good provider. Easier following you around than fishing himself."

"I think I will go lie down," Mary said.

First Snow

The trees had been bare for weeks. Rain, wind and cold that followed and never left, drained all brightness from the autumn foliage, turned the leaves to sere, brown ancient things. Dead leaves that blew in the early night pecking winter's warning against windowpanes, then swirled down empty sidewalks until rain turned them to sodden sludge. Away from towns and villages, the blowing leaves flew across fields and pastures, caught at woods' edges and settled with the season's final sighing goodbye. Even the tamarac were done. Proud gold torches for a week bordering the edges of evergreen forest or rimming backwoods ponds, now their needles were going fast. Great voids appeared among their branches, giving them the look of Christmas trees tossed on a dump. The naked hardwoods were gray on gray — some silk, some smokey-dull depending on whether you saw them from a distance or fairly close, or were looking at the fine branch networks or the trunks.

The first snow changed everything. It came in the night, a heavy wet snow that would not last, but did good things while it was here. It took away the look of flatness and gave the country dimension and light. On the flat flood plain beside the river there lay a flawless white coat. Thirty yards inland was a break of dark trees, then the harvested hay or corn fields, emerging stubble against white giving the open expanse a textured appearance all the way to the road.

Driving slowly, I passed yesterday's dooryard litter of junk, today looking like an outdoor antique mart. Farm equipment, wrecked cars, an old wagon wheel, a canvas-covered boat upon a trailer, lay draped with the snow's white mantel. A yellow dog trotted carefully around the transformed objects raising feet high, leaving round dark holes. Cows, black and white, walked along the barbed-wire fences.

The river went slowly down and emptied into the lake beneath a small bridge. There was a turnoff for parking just before the bridge, and standing there now in the quiet with the engine stopped, I could hear snow dropping slushy soft from telephone wires. It was a short walk down to the bridge past big maples, their trunks dark wet on one side where snow had blown, stuck, then melted. There would be no sun, that was plain, but the snow-brightness was such a change you no longer minded. The river flowed slowly under the bridge, emptying into the lake which opened and stretched, to the north, long and gray with blue-white snow-covered hills and mountains in the distance. There was a high rounded lookout point on the far side of the bridge, a curving rock and gravel shore on the side where I stood. The air was so clean and cold after the snow, breathing it was more like drinking crystal-clear spring water.

Around the lookout point a small flock of mallards worked my way. The water, pushing around rocks and the bank, had that thick look it gets just before it freezes. Just out from the bridge in midstream, the water surface suddenly popped and broke. I saw it from the corner of my eye and quickly turned toward the rings spreading slowly, in perfect concentricity, in the thick water. They were still spreading when the fish, or another, rose again, splitting the surface with the dark edge of its dorsal fin. Everywhere else the water was flat and silvery. Of course I walked back to the truck, rummaged under the cap, found the box with streamers, and took the rod that was in the overhead rack, still with its reel in place. I knew it would take longer to rerig back there with the tension from the nearness of the fish, but I went back anyway. I strung the rod in the cold and tied on the fly. There was no sign of the fish.

Standing on the bank on the near side of the bridge, I shook out some line, made several quick false casts, stripping fast from the reel, and sent the streamer toward the place where the fish had been. Just casting again was wonderful. The line landed light and straight, making a slim razor slice in the surface. I saw that most of the ducks had come around the point, hugging it close. They were in grand shape, full, round and smooth-looking, floating lightly.

The streamer darted through the place where the rises had come, and now I slid the line across the water, quickly lifting it high and back, stripping more from the reel, then shooting it all out over the water.

The fish broke water again. It was about as far as I had cast, but towards the far side of the river and the point. It was only a dark glint, something that could have been imagined, but the widening rings of the rise were still there to show I had not been mistaken. The streamer was dark green, white and blue with a hint of pink and fine Mylar ribbons to look like the little smelt the fish had fed upon all fall. I brought it in fast, skimming the surface, then lifted it out and cast where the fish had rolled. The streamer hit the surface like a single raindrop. I let it sink just a little, then made quick little strips, imagining it darting, fluttering down there in the cold. On the next strip it stopped and the line was tight for a moment against my hand and the bowed rod, before whispering out through the guides. It took perhaps two seconds before the fish jumped, heavy and all silvery. No thick-bodied smallmouth as I suspected, but one of the lake's big rainbows that had come to this shallow end of the lake to feed in the cold water, perhaps to stay through winter until spring ice-out.

It ran fast and hard, jumped twice more before giving me a chance to begin reeling. The trout fought in the deeper water of the channel carved by the river outflow, keeping my rod bent, sending the tangible story of its throbbing struggle back to both my hands. Then, diabolically, with all that open water behind, the fish made a terrible move for me. It ran for the river. It came fast, straight for the bridge, and I scrabbled along the bank, kicking down little stones toward the ducks. The hen on the rock raised her head in alarm, and the birds in the water eased a little way from shore. I ran for the bridge.

The trout made it there and was under the bridge before me. My flyline rubbed against the concrete abutment. I ran, thrusting the rod ahead like a javelin to clear the line. The trout leaped on the far side of the bridge. I saw him while hanging over the abutment, looking through; saw him framed within the bridge and diorama darkness inside the structure. Then the big rainbow stalled. I took the moment, pumping the rod, reeling with hands outstretched over the river. Some of the ducks moved along the shore watching, maybe trusting that I would soon toss them something edible, maybe just curious.

The trout started back. It chose to come under the bridge, running just past me before leaping again. All the while I tried to keep up with it, keep as little slack as possible from forming in the line. I was almost successful. When the rainbow came out of the water on that return run, he was not very far away and it was easy to see how thick and fat he was from feeding on young smelt. Sleek and fat and in fine condition from the cold water. He would weigh six, maybe seven pounds. But he was slowing. I could hold him in the middle of the river, despite the steady current. I canted the rod over, trying to turn his head, move him from the flow, dominate him. He began to come.

He came perhaps fifteen feet before turning for the river channel once more, taking a little line. I gave it, but he earned every inch, and when he stalled I turned him again. A pod of four mallards, all drakes, left the flock, paddling in the general direction of the fish. They left a little vee wake in the thick silky water. The big rainbow came to the surface and boiled, showing his bright olive back and broad tail, before slanting a few feet down again. The line was off the water. Only the clear monofilament leader cut the surface, making little zig-zag movements through the water, following the fish's erratic surges for freedom.

The lead drake broke from the others, turned for the place where the trout wallowed near the surface.

"Hey," I yelled, "get out of there!"

The duck kept swimming. It swam beneath the leader, eyeing the little darting pattern the mono made as it cut the water. I raised my rod to keep the leader from brushing the drake's back. I chose my comments to the drake with care. Then I gave the fish some slack, hoping it would move away. It did.

The trout swam slowly back to the middle of the river channel, into the current, leaving the mallard behind. When I tightened up on the fish, the current against it brought the leader down on a more acute angle to the water's surface. The drake came back. He swam quickly, obviously excited, totally disregarding my cries. The knot tying the butt section to the

transition section of the mono leader was perhaps a foot above the water. It was a very small, neat knot except for the strand of green vegetation it had picked up somewhere while my fish made its fight. The big, bright drake did not hesitate. When he was close enough, he stretched surely, opened a bill only slightly paler orange than his bright legs and feet, and nibbled the little flag of green that grew from my leader. It was really not a violent thing. I felt it all the while, quick little bouncy vibrations. But it was more than the leader could stand, and the heaviness that was my fine rainbow trout, suddenly was gone.

The duck made his kick-up, flapped his wings showing the pretty blue speculum, then tipped over and shot his curly tail in the air in final salute. I returned one of mine, reeled in the empty line, and stood there. If you believed in omens, it was past time to call it a season. Besides, the trout season had been closed for a week.

You would have released the fish, anyway, consoled the inner voice while I walked alone to the truck.

"Of course," I said.

Then why were you fishing?

"Why do I ever fish? To fish!"

Is it allowed? I mean to fish for them when the season's closed?

"It could have been a bass, or even a *perch*. Besides, a rise is a rise."

Didn't you see that first fish was a trout?

"I don't think so."

Are you sure?

" — —."

Well, you may have been right. Maybe you didn't see. Sort of ironic about the duck, eh? No need to make a decision at all.

"Listen, I said there wasn't a question . . ."

Oh, I believe you. Just doing a little needling. Turned out a nice day after all, didn't it?

"I think I'll go south," I said.

The Singing Waters May Make You Scream

The two men started up the long and treeless hill that began just behind the last street of the settlement. Beyond the crest of the hill was a gentle dip and rise, and then the land swept open, stretched on as far as you could see, high, stark, rolling hills. They called it The Country.

Lichens clung where they could survive on the protected sides of rocks, and mosses grew in the rock niches. This high and exposed to the wind, there were no lush blankets of pale, gray-green caribou moss. The walking was not difficult, but the abrasiveness of the black rock would be very rough on a hiker's footwear. The younger man, whose name was Adrian Wells, hoped that tomorrow the weather would lift and their flight would take them from this place to the camp on the river. It was his first time in the North Country.

"I was stranded here almost a week, once," said his companion, Mike Shepard. "But I don't look for that to happen now. I was too early in the year, then."

Across the folds of rolling hills, there were long, narrow caribou trails, carved and pounded, never varying, from uncounted years of migrations. Out to the left was the river turning to estuary, flowing to the great bay and the ocean beyond.

"How far a walk is it out there?" Adrian asked.

"Not too bad. It's something to do."

They looked down on the settlement. The litter of trash and oil drums behind many of the simple dwellings and Quonset huts did not look as bad from this distance.

"Well, that's the view," Mike said. "You ready to go back?"

"Sure. Then I guess I'll walk around awhile," Adrian said.

They cut in back of the white-steepled church, its paint peeling, and once they were on the primary road Shepard stopped.

"I'll go see what everyone's doing — or if there's any late weather news," he said. "We'll either be in the saloon or back at the Quonset hut. You won't get lost."

"See you later," said Adrian.

He watched his friend walk down the unpaved road, then turned in the opposite direction, passing the picket fence in front of the church where children played in the yard dirt. He cut down another road going by the native community center, then the liquor authority building with clearly printed white signs announcing the weekly beer ration reduction for each man and woman in the settlement. A cooperative government-native council effort, the signs stated. One step down the long road to sobriety was the implication.

Two more blocks and he was in front of the Old Com-

pany store. He climbed the gray, weathered steps, remembering how veterans of the North described the company — the devil incarnate. Over a century-and-a-half of luring the native peoples in from the country; building dependence on trade; nurturing the natural desire for creature comforts from the south; bonding the early trappers and fishermen — both natives and pioneering families alike — with extended credit for supplies in return for regulated fur prices. It was good business.

Inside, he found a jammed array of foodstuffs, hardware, clothing, toys, luxury items, native crafts — a kind of early 1900s general store. There was no background music or computerized checkout equipment. The clerk was a pale, loose-fleshed woman without expression. He browsed and went out. On the steps an Inuit or Indian — he could not yet tell — stopped him. The man looked about twenty, his eyes glassy and unfocused. He worked for balance on the steps.

"Hey, man," he said. "You got any dope?"

"No," Adrian told him, starting down.

"No?" The young man was disbelieving. "No? Nothing?"

Adrian shook his head again, gained the road and headed toward the houses on the lower settlement edge, past which the land opened going toward the estuary. He walked by a number of square, prefabricated dwellings. At one corner, the remains of a home still smoldered from the fire which had recently destroyed it. A number of people poked through the rubble. A man pulled a mattress with only one corner burned from a section of the dwelling that still stood.

At another corner two native girls lounged against a faded yellow structure. They wore tight, rock-hero clothing and garish masks of makeup. They smiled at him and one of them beckoned.

"Hey, come over here," she said.

Adrian waved noncommittedly and continued on the little road.

That night the weather lifted. In the morning the sun cracked the gray cloud banks while they ate hurriedly. Excitement building, they flung equipment, then themselves, into a truck and rolled for the airport. Their equipment was transferred to the fat-bellied Canso for the flight in.

Hatches slammed with thudding finality. Seconds later the twin engines revved to a deafening level, and the old aircraft rattled down the short runway, lifting quickly. The plane banked and straightened, heading west, the engine level dropping to a thought-destroying drone. If you yelled loudly enough it was possible to make yourself understood over the sound.

They flew in from the coast, reaching the big river and the border of the northern treeline. There were vast open stretches of tundra, of rolling subarctic vegetation meeting stands of spruce in curving ribbons the way surf climbs a sand beach. From the air the river was broad, mostly flat, bending gently, studded with wrinkled sections that marked the rapids. They banked, and the camp buildings lay below along one shore like little Monopoly game structures. There was a long stretch of smooth, broad water before the camp and they came in over the trees, dropping fast, touching down on the first approach in a double smack and rush of water beneath the floats. They motored toward the buoy-marked anchorage just off shore and Adrian saw the big freighter canoes coming out to meet them.

The unloading of men and equipment went quickly. The guides and Inuit camp owner held their boats steady below the plane. Returning to shore, the canoes were pulled part way up peeled log ramps. Rough logs nailed crossways between poles formed the walkways connecting the camp service buildings and the wood-frame sleeping cabins, keeping you off the spongy-wet earth. Beyond the camp cluster, narrow trails cut back into the country through pale gray-green caribou moss. Adrian shouldered a bag and headed to the cabin where he'd been assigned with the others.

The cabin slept six in bunk beds, and they were five. They unpacked, rigged rods and stowed them horizontally on nails on the outside walls of the cabins. They ate dinner in a separate building. There was thick well-flavored stew with fresh bread and fruit pies for desert. A dozen condiments clustered on the oilcloth in the middle of the long tables. It was late when they finished, and they had time only to fish the long, broad home pool. One angler jumped a salmon. Two others took good brook trout near tributary mouths, and that was all. In the morning they would travel the river far up or down stream, passing through rapids with the jet-drive outboards, trusting their lives to mechanical performance and the boat-handling skill of the guides.

Retiring to their cabin, the men lit Coleman lanterns, broke out a deck of cards and a bottle of fine single malt. Adrian surveyed the men with whom he'd shared the flight from Montreal. There was his friend Mike Shephard; Jack Ryan, a loquacious redhead; Edeas, a thin old Frenchman from Quebec; and Ken Thompson, part Inuit, from a long line of trappers and settlers in this country. Ken Thompson was an elected representative of the territory. Not really of the group of anglers, he was on a kind of working holiday, visiting the native-run outfitting operations the government helped finance, talking with his constituents, and hopeful of getting in a little fishing at the same time.

They passed the bottle. It was inevitable that the stories would soon follow. At first, there were the tales of big fish, lost fish, great hunts. Then, slowly, they began to change. The cards snapped and rattled on the wood table in the harsh glare of the lanterns. Adrian found himself listening to descriptions of a world he thought existed lifetimes ago. What unfolded was very much alive, and he was on its threshold here. Old Edeas was full of himself recounting escapes from rapids, near freezings, of men gone mad from isolation and the torture of insect swarms that filled their eyes, ears and nostrils, and then their mouths when they opened them to scream. But beyond the failures of mechanical equipment, the miscalculations of men, the strandings, the hope or resignation of the lost and starving, was the presence of the country. It seemed to loom there, overpoweringly. Adrian thought briefly of his own world — in travel time, not very far away at all. Just outside the cabin was all the difference.

Mike Shepard gathered in the cards for the next deal. "You know," he said, "we get a pretty good feel for things traveling around here in the easy time. It's the thought of getting through an entire winter here without support that's frightening." He looked at Ken Thompson. "It's people like your folks and their friends — all the early settlers in this country — who really know. What a thing it must be." He began dealing the cards.

Ken smiled a little, nodded. He reached for the bottle, poured himself a short drink. "They went through a lot," he said. "It was hard enough for the trappers on their lines, but you've got to imagine the loneliness of their wives and children. Three months at a time alone in the cabins. No mail. Never an idea if the men were still alive. Or dying. Or gone. Just those isolated cabins with the wolves passing by, and the darkness. So much of the time, in darkness."

He sipped slowly, placed his glass on a hard reel box on the floor, and leaned his chair back on two legs. He sat apart from the players near the wood stove, back out of the direct light, shadows accentuating his high cheekbones. He ran fingers of one hand through dark straight hair, looking at the card players but going inside himself.

"My mother and father went through it. So did my brothers and sisters. And that wasn't very long ago." He did not add himself. "I can tell you something about the winter. It's one of the saddest stories, though." He paused a moment, then continued. "This was a family like ours. The man had come out of the country and sold his furs. It was the end of January. He was to go back in a month, of course, for the second half of the trapping, but his wife was near to giving birth. She had not been well at all, then suddenly became very sick. There were no doctors in the bush, but in a settlement some hours away by sled, there was a nurse. His wife's pain had become terrible and the trapper made the decision to go for help, to bring the nurse. He left his fourteen-year-old daughter to keep the fire going, and struck out with the team and kamutick — the sled with the box — so he could carry the nurse. The weather was all right. No one could have predicted what was coming — it came so fast.

"It was a freak storm, a terrible storm, and the snow came pounding heavy — more than forty inches of it. The man was in it and right behind the snow came the freeze. He could tell how bad the cold was going to be the way the temperature dropped so fast. They say if it gets cold enough it cannot snow, but that's untrue. He was half way and had to make the decision to continue or return to his family. He decided it would go worse for them if he was dead, so he turned back. Going across the mouth of a river in the storm, he broke through and went part way into the water. He had to work fast now, to knock all snow and water from his feet and legs so they would not freeze. The kamutik was wet, too, and by the time he had cleared his feet and got the sled away from the wet, it was heavy, too frozen to be pulled.

"He unhitched the dogs and traveled on, walking. He was worried that his feet had become wet, but it was so cold the water had frozen on the outside of his boots before it was able to soak through. He had beaten most of it off but still the snow and ice crusted around his boots and lower legs, always building, weighing him down. The temperature fell to forty-five below that night. He had to stop several times to try to thaw his face, but he reached the cabin.

"He stumbled in, covered with ice and snow, and inside the cabin all was frozen. His daughter lay huddled on the floor where she had fallen asleep trying and failing to keep the fire going. His wife was frozen in her bed. She was dead. And the poor girl. So cold; it was so terribly cold. Her legs were frozen from her feet to just above the knees, but she was still alive. He was like an ice creature himself, his clothes all frozen and cracking as he moved, but he had no time to lose, and he had no choice. He told us how he cried and the tears froze to his face while he cut off the poor girl's legs.

"He jammed her into the flour barrel and the flour stemmed the bleeding while he tore all cloth he could find in the cabin, ripping like a madman to make the bandages. The girl lived. She lived in the settlement after that, and in following years traveled with a mission raising money for crippled people of the territory. They raised millions. They finally gave her artificial limbs for her work. She was in her eighties when she died."

The men at the table continued to face Thompson after the story was over. The cards were still.

"God, what a thing," Jack Ryan said. He poured from the bottle and passed it. Sitting on his bunk, Adrian could see Ken Thompson was remembering something else. Mike Shepard passed his hand over his cards, spreading them a little, gathering them.

"Some survived the winter with even less than a cabin," Thompson began again. "My father and older brother, who was sixteen at the time, had the job of bringing out the canoes of the other trappers that summer. Someone always took that job. Then all the trappers would not have to go in for their canoes. They were paid, of course, but it was a long, hard job. They had eleven canoes to bring out. Once they reached the trapping territory there were many miles to cover. The lines of each man were spread to work a different area, and his canoe had been left where he had first gone in. In the end, it would be a seven-hundred-mile trip that took six weeks. There were big portages, too, and rapids to run.

"While on one of the portages around a falls, my father and brother met an Indian family who had wintered over. There was a six-year-old-boy, the wife who was pregnant, and the man. Their shelter was a tattered tent pocked with holes and old fish netting whose meshes had been filled with spruce bows. They lived all winter in that, and the reason for it was the man heard he was wanted in connection with a murder in the large settlement, and he fled with his family. In fact, he was just wanted as a witness, but he had been afraid, and never knew. His friends were to come in that fall either to get him, or to bring more supplies if the family had to stay. But now the family was out of food and the man had run out of ammunition for his rifle.

"My father and brother had two geese and gave the man one. My father went up to portage the last canoe and while he was gone, the man tried to sneak the other goose from my brother. My father returned just in time. They needed that goose, themselves. My father understood how badly off the family was, though. After seeing they both had rifles of the same caliber, my father gave the man the seven cartridges he had left. It was a very small caliber, I think maybe a twenty-five Stevens. Then my father and brother continued down-river, bringing the canoes.

"After they ate their goose, they were out of food, too. They couldn't leave the canoes. The canoes had been promised. They also meant the money for the winter trapping supplies. But near the river there were raspberries. My father and brother lived on the berries for three days, running and portaging the canoes. Finally they reached the last trapper's cabin where there was some food, and then they were all right. They had some bad rapids to run the last seventy-five miles, but they made them, losing only one small canoe which swamped.

"Late that fall some friends of that Indian family came 'round to my father's cabin. They came to thank my father. They told him that with those seven cartridges the man had killed eight caribou. They had the meat, the hides and leather for clothing, and the family got through fine. And the trouble at the settlement was over.

"That was some time ago, of course," Thompson added.

"But not all that long. Things are a lot easier now. In some ways. But the country — they haven't changed the country very much. You don't have to go very far."

"Not so far," Edeas agreed. "Even with all they put underwater with their dams. It's just waiting for them. They leave any of it alone too long and the water and weather will take it back, you'll see."

He tapped the table. The men examined their cards, and the game began again.

I t was late, the card game over when Adrian went outside. He walked to a lookout above the river. In the bright moonlight the tops of the spruce trees were silhouetted on the banks high above the river. Below him the water was shrouded in darkness, but downstream the moonlight touched it, glittering on its surface. The river flowed smoothly with heavy current. The brightness of the moon diminished the stars near it, but away over the darkened camp buildings, the sky was so choked by starlight that familiar constellations seemed superimposed upon strange new ones, on and on without end, far beyond his ability to see. And spreading in all directions from the tenuous claim the camp had made upon its wildness, was the country.

Returning to the cabin he remembered the squalor and despair of the settlement where they had spent the previous night, and wondered what would lure a person from the open land to that gray and constricted existence. Perhaps the empty promise of easier life. Or maybe it was something else; something that he would discover building his own memories. He thought again of Ken Thompson's stories, trusting, as he entered the cabin, that their adventures this trip would prove a good deal milder. There was one lantern burning low inside. He undressed, then turned the valve knob clockwise. The hissing of the gas vapor stopped, the flame guttered and died. In darkness he found his bunk.

Billy Uptik was their guide. The young Inuit was comfortable speaking English, enthused with his job, with the fish, wildlife and the land. He handled their equipment carefully, commenting knowledgeably on a high-quality rod, reel or gear bag.

"I have new place," he told them. "We walk, then take one canoe I have far down." He waved an arm toward the river. "But it's a very good place. Salmon come up from rapids, rest in smooth water. Many fish. OK?"

"How far?" Mike Shepard asked.

"Maybe one, one-and-a-half hour. Little more."

Shepard looked at Adrian. "Cuts into the fishing time," he said, "but Billy knows his stuff. If you don't mind the extra trip."

"Fine," Adrian said.

Billy nodded, shouldered his pack, took two of their rods and one gear bag, and headed down to the river. Two in a canoe, the other guests were heading to various upriver pools and lies. Billy's canoe had no jet-drive outboard.

"Short trip, first," he said, seeing Shepard notice.

They quartered cross river to a gravel point on the far shore, beached the boat, climbed out. A piled stone *inukshuk* marked the narrow trail head. They started up the steep slope away from the river. The trail rose, leveled, climbed again, then leveled off. They were at the height of land where in another age the river had first flowed and begun its timeless carving through the natural drop of land and rock. The trail was narrow, cut through caribou moss, low scrub spruce.

There were other strangely shaped mosses, lichens, and here and there dots of some red-leaved plant adding counterpoint to the subtle shades of gray, green and brown. Once Adrian saw tiny yellow flowers growing in the protected lee of a dwarf tree.

They walked quickly, maintaining the bouncy cross-country step that ate up miles. After a time they broke from the heavier stands of stunted trees. From the trail they could just see a glint of the river, and wanting the view, walked to the edge of the canyon rim through untracked caribou moss, crushing it underfoot, making tracks that would last a very long time. The river stretched below.

Finally, they reached the river and found the canoe with a jet-drive engine that Billy had left there. They loaded quickly, Billy holding the boat in the shallows while they climbed in. It was good to rest, though it was to be short lived.

The river was swift here. They ran the main channel, Uptik sitting happily at the tiller, looking ahead. They swept past huge, gray, widely scattered boulders that broke the current, soon coming to an old burn on the far shore, the still-standing skeletons of destroyed spruce charred and lonely on the high bank. Where a thick forest had once been, new low growth had begun, covering most of the blackened remains left by the fire. Overhead, great gray clouds rolled on endlessly, and suddenly they were aware that the river had quickened.

Where the heavy current had once split around the rocks and boulders, it now hit and sometimes combed over them. They looked ahead and saw the river had gone white.

"We're going *through* that?" Adrian yelled over the engine noise.

"I guess," Shepard said. "Trust Billy, he's good."

The sound of the water grew swiftly, overpowering the engine. Then they were in the rapids, the thundering roar surrounding them. From a small, clean slicing missile, the boat became a pitching shell that leaped in the troubled water, yawed suddenly, then regained balance. Adrian glanced at Billy, saw the seriousness of the young guide's face framed by his rainjacket hood just before the first wave jumped the port bow gunwale and smacked them. He turned ahead again and wondered if there was hope.

The big canoe rose and slammed. Pillowed water warned of rocks hidden just below the surface. Billy easily avoided them, aimed for a stretch of angrily standing haystack wave formations. The boat sliced through prettily, rushed on in the maelstrom of seething water. Ahead there was a nest of great jagged rocks followed by a garage-size boulder. Opposite the great boulder the water curled from a hideous length of knife-edge ledging. The river smashed insanely, leaped what obstacles it could, fell back on itself in maddened search for passage. One small deep-water channel passed through it all, and Billy Uptik fought the canoe toward it.

The river had them, took them rushingly into the compressed slot between ledge and boulder, solid wall of rock suddenly on the left, the ledge rising wraithlike, a headland in pounding surf, touching close. Then they were out, dancing through a garden of round-domed rocks, and they had made it. The water was still fast but the river widened, beginning to quiet while the rocks trickled away and the bottom deepened. Adrian felt the tendons of his forearms aching from his grip on the seat, tried to uncurl fingers that clutched like talons turned to iron.

Uptik grinned broadly, water dripping from his nose and chin.

"Scare you?" he asked.

"Yes," Adrian told him. He looked at his friend. "How about getting back?"

"That's what the jet drive is for." Mike said. "Don't think about it."

"Through *that*?" Adrian asked incredulously.

"He'll try. How else? Look at those banks."

The banks of the river were steep and ragged. It would

be impossible to drag a boat back along shore. Still, the camp boat had been there waiting for them. Obviously he must have run this sector before — and perhaps more importantly, made it back.

The river moved with dignity now, carrying them in a long, sweeping bend around a high, broken point. Past it, the banks suddenly slouched, hunching off into broad shores. Small, smooth rocks and flat stone shingles formed the beaches. Scrub willows grew just above. Ahead was a small island in mid-river, and there was something in the river swimming toward it from the left bank.

"Caribou?" Mike said.

"Maybe," Billy told him. "But no antlers."

They could see the animal's head moving steadily just above the surface, rising as it gained the shallows, clawed the rocky bottom and began climbing out.

"It's a wolf!" Adrian exclaimed. "A timber wolf!"

The animal heaved itself from the river, growing larger as they closed on it, growing huge. It was pale gray, and it shook itself like a dog. They could see the water spraying from its pelt. It trotted across the island, dropped into the river on the other side, swimming again, holding itself well going across the current. They were close now. The big wolf reached the right shore, rose from the water, shaking itself once more. Then it turned and looked at them with terribly bright eyes, and Adrian thought he had never seen such an indifferent stare from an animal. The wolf turned and loped ahead in great distance-eating strides, ghosting off into the spruce for-

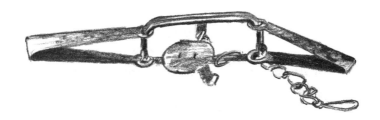

est that began back from the river. They looked at Billy, who was nodding his head silently.

The river turned again, and around the bend was a little slough. The guide headed the boat for it, slid the bow in, and they were out, pulling the canoe up the beach.

"This is place for fishing." Billy said. "Have to check water now."

They walked the shore out toward the low point that backed up the slough, crossed it and were beside the main river. The guide pointed at the long, slick pool in mid-river. The pool dropped over a sharp lip into another rapids, as long and as powerful as they had already run.

"Fish here." Billy pointed out into the pool. "Good water."

"How do you reach it?" Adrian asked.

"Fish in boat," said the guide. "Up close." He motioned to the drop before the rapids.

Shepard looked at the white water carefully. "I'm glad he doesn't plan to run this one. I don't think it's passable. You'd have to line a boat through."

Billy walked back to the beach and picked up two skull-size rocks. He placed them in the boat, then looked for another. The one he chose was slightly larger.

"Anchor," he explained. "Better get rods ready now."

"What fly do they like here?" Shepard asked the guide.

"Salmon flies or big streamers. Black ghost. Muddler fly. Any fly they eat here."

"We could use a few cooperative salmon once in awhile." Shepard tied on a big, bright Durham Ranger.

"I'll go dull, then." Adrian said. He selected a large double hook salmon muddler and tied it on.

Billy waded into the shallows with his anchor rocks and placed them gently in the canoe. He tied a bow line to one of the medium-size rocks, tightening his knots carefully. Then he lowered the anchor into the bow, waded out a little, and climbed in. Adrian rolled over the gunwale to sit in the bow, while Mike held the boat amidships until the engine was started. Then he quickly hopped in.

They nosed out into the heavy current.

"Get anchor ready," Billy said. Adrian bent for the rock anchor. Holding it, he leaned out over the bow. They were at the head of the big, slick pool and could see well down into the dark, amber water. The flow was quiet but strong and steady here. They clearly heard the growling rapids below, and it was some seconds later that Adrian realized the reason for it. Uptik had killed the engine. Adrian jerked around, saw the guide gesturing violently.

"Drop anchor!" Billy said urgently.

Adrian had already let it go. He felt it thump the bottom, commence bumping as it dragged along.

"Holding?" inquired the guide.

"No," Adrian told him. "Not holding."

The freighter canoe drifted slowly toward the dropoff. Adrian clutched the anchor line as though he were strangling it.

"Still not holding," he told Billy.

Several side currents now gathered together and the boat slipped back with greater speed. Adrian saw Mike grab both gunwales.

"Not holding!" Adrian warned again. "Can't we get out of here . . ."

They were sweeping backwards swiftly now, toward the lip of the pool and the dropoff that would send them into the violence below.

"Wait 'til close," Billy told them. "No scaring fish with engine."

"Still *not holding*!" yelled Adrian, the sound of the rapids below surrounded them. Then Billy yanked the engine's starter cord. The engine coughed and died. All the anchor line was out now, but the boat continued drifting. Billy yanked the starter rope a second time. They were drifting very fast, and the engine coughed twice on the second pull, then was quiet. On the third try the engine started and Billy slammed it into gear. They moved ahead, water sweeping powerfully past the hull, Adrian hauling line hand over hand and dropping it into the boat. Shepard stared back in horror at the lip they had approached to within two lengths of their fishing rods. Then he turned and looked at Adrian sitting in the bow, face lifted to the sky, saying nothing.

They made a wide circle to avoid motoring through the pool, and this time Uptik chose a spot slightly off-center of the mid-river current before shutting down the engine. Adrian already had the larger rock tied to the anchor line. He jettisoned it the moment the engine died.

Line shot roughly through his hands. He felt the bump, when the rock hit, then another as he let out more line to bring the anchor back to the bottom. "Not holding," he said. He let out all the line right away, stopped it, felt the rock catch once, break free and drag a little before it jammed solidly. "Holding," he announced. He kept a deathgrip on the line, feeling it hum in the current. The anchor held. "Still holding," he said with relief. The canoe swung around and stopped, well-placed at the head of the pool.

Billy nodded, smiling. "OK," he told them. "Fish here."

"Provided we stop twitching enough to cast," Shepard said. Billy looked at him questioningly. "Close," Mike told him, pointing to the rapids, then holding his hands separated by six inches.

Billy nodded, smiling. "Yes," he said. "Good thing engine start."

Adrian waved his rod tip, shaking out line. "These fish must hole up after making that run. But the current's pretty strong here, too."

"Not as bad as that," Shepard pointed toward the rapids with his rod.

They began alternating casts, Adrian toward the shore from which they had come, Shepard toward the center of the river. The flies made long swings down and then across stream, covering more of the pool as they lengthened their casts. It was near the completion of one of these swings that Adrian's line stopped and darted forward. There was no hesitation, just a violent tightening of the line. He had no time or need to strike. The salmon rushed straightaway, then came up as they shouted.

It went into the air in a series of jumps, its head curving over toward its tail, sometimes hanging with the odd stillness of a rocket whose power is suddenly disrupted, before resuming the violent head shake as it crashed back in. They could see how dark its color was. It was nearly as dark as a kelt, winter-gaunt on its river descent to feed, heal and strengthen in the sea, but this was no spent salmon. The fish was on its spawning run, so long in fresh water, so far from the estuary and the ocean, that it had lost its silver. None of its strength.

Adrian fought the salmon with great concentration, ignoring their comments. When he brought it in the first time, Billy was ready with the big-hoop net, but the salmon bulled away, heading back to the spot where it had taken the fly. He changed angles and slowly coaxed it from the lie. The fish shot ahead, upstream, then swept down toward them, Adrian reeling frantically, lifting his rod to add the last needed bit of pressure to bring the fish close enough. Billy took it in the net as it tried to sweep past.

"Good fish! Nice Job!" Shepard exclaimed. "What a jumper he was! Or she. Nope, a he."

Billy removed the salmon from the meshes. Its hooked kype jutted fiercely. The guide killed the fish without asking.

"Catch a fish, will you," Adrian said.

Shepard obliged.

After that, there was no keeping track of hookups, jumped fish, boated fish. It was that fast. It was too fast to be salmon fishing, but it was. It was incredible. Clippers, tippet spools, pieces of leader fell to the bottom of the canoe following hurried effort to repair terminal tackle. At one point Shepard broke his big rod. He switched to a lighter trout rod.

It did not matter. He still took fish, though beating them took slightly longer.

"The bottom must be paved with them!" Adrian said. "I've never seen salmon like this." Shepard started to reply, but his reel interrupted, ratcheting in high decibels as a fish hit and continued running. Uptik was in a near perpetual dance, swinging side to side, scooping, netting, sometimes missing, removing hooks. The canoe bottom was wet from fish and the dripping net. They did not stop to eat sandwiches they had brought. They fished until their hands swelled and grew cold.

"Your arms and shoulders feel like mine?" Adrian asked finally.

"Probably worse," Mike said.

They paused, resting their rods in the boat, resting from the nonstop casting, and improbable number of fought fish. For the last hour, Billy Uptik had been checking the sky. Now he scanned it again, finding the brightest area where the sun burned behind curtains of cloud layers.

"Got to go," said Billy Uptik.

They broke their rods, cased them in the aluminum tubes and stowed them in the bottom of the big canoe. The guide was uneasy. You could see it in his nervous movements, the way he tugged at the drawstring of his rainjacket hood, the continued fussing with equipment already well secured in the boat. Adrian could feel the tension building. He looked at Shepard, who nodded once, and he knew his friend was feeling the same thing.

"OK," Billy said. He pulled the starter cord. The engine caught on the first try.

Adrian grabbed at the anchor line, hauling quickly, dropping it in the bow followed by the rock anchor. He wiped his hands roughly on his trousers, yanked up the zipper of his raincoat, checked the fasteners of his life jacket. Then he turned to face what was coming.

In a moment they were out of the heavy-smooth flow of the pool and into bouncy water that hurried over shallow stones and gravel. Without the jet drive they would not have been able to navigate the shallows, nor would they be able to survive farther upriver where a standard propellor could quickly smash itself useless on hidden boulders. Several times the engine's lower unit struck and dragged through the gravel and rock of the bottom. They ran quickly, easily through the small peaked waves into heavier water, entering the field of rounded rocks where the river was still wide but the current much heavier. It slid thick and glassy around the smooth, immovable rock domes rising like skulls through the surface. The endless rush of water was dangerously hypnotic. It was far too easy to watch it overlong and lose concentration on the essential job of picking the passable route far enough ahead.

The engine was still powerful enough to move them steadily into the current. Uptik held them mid-river, threading a course around the rocks with quick movements of the tiller, sudden bursts with the throttle. The boat responded quickly, agily. Then Adrian allowed himself the long look ahead. In horror he turned back toward Shepard and the guide whose eyes were locked on the river unaware he had ever turned. He wanted to leave the boat.

Ahead, the banks suddenly closed, constricting the violent flow with jagged walls, and they could see the steepness of the gradient. The river angled up in the kind of swath cut by a lava flow in the side of a mountain, and the water thundered down. A plume of white shot, as though turbine-discharged, through the narrow passage between ledge and boulder where they'd passed earlier.

Shepard fidgeted with the zipper of his life jacket, shoved

one knee to the bottom of the boat, looking ready to spring. Then the guide twisted the throttle and the canoe leaped ahead. They were in it, and the booming roar of the river consumed them. It was more than sound. It filled their minds and lungs, humming deeply through their being. The boat bucked and dropped in the violence of waves that cleaved on boulders, smashed together in endless wrenching, opposing force.

Wave tops leaped the gunwales, raking, stinging their faces. In the bow, Adrian was getting the worst of the pounding. Once a trough opened deeply before them, and for a moment they were suspended. Then they fell, striking the water again painfully hard. As they dropped, the anchor rock smashed against Adrian's ankle. The hurt seemed a very distant thing. Just ahead, the surface parted fleetingly, long enough to show the wrinkled rock edge directly in their path. Adrian opened his mouth to shout the warning. A curling tongue of water hit the port bow and kept coming into his face, filling his mouth, choking his breath.

Billy had seen it, too. He jammed the tiller nearly full over, throttling up, then straightening it almost immediately as the boat yawed dangerously. Coughing the inhaled water, Adrian half turned, seeing Shepard kneeling in water, scanning the river wildly. The guide crouched, knees bent, a fierceness in his face. They approached the mouth of the slot between the ledge and wall-like boulder where the constricted water thundered at them. Billy nosed the boat into each momentary weakness of current that allowed them to move forward. Then they held, not losing or gaining, the river pounding around them.

Shepard stared at the engine and Adrian suddenly realized that the guide had the throttle wide open. The engine was unable to move them against the current. They held, Billy weaving the tiller, waiting like salmon holding with all their power, seeking each tiny lessening of flow that allowed them to dart a short way forward again. There was a glassy pocket now, and the boat slid into it, holding once more, Adrian trying to count off seconds, trying anything. They held, it seemed forever, and he realized his count meant five minutes stalled in the roaring madness. Wall-like, a single wave reared and blanketed the boulder, angling off it across their bow. The river seemed to hold its breath, and they were moving forward through the slot, moving slowly. Moving. They were through.

The guide wrenched the boat out of the main flow into a secondary current. They moved faster, away from the nightmare passage, leaving it behind. The river was still rapids, ripping crazily from containment by the high-walled banks, but they were going through it. The side current held and Billy followed it, working around the pillowed rocks, the jagged boulders and through two sets of peaked and dancing waves. They hit something just once, scraping and dragging a hundred feet above the passage, and then the engine coughed, caught, sputtered — and died.

The canoe began turning stern angling out, back toward the main channel, bow swinging. Shepard scrambled in the wet and debris on the bottom, coming up with a paddle, yelling at the guide, who wheeled, yanking frantically at the starter cord. In the tangled anchor rope Adrian saw the handle of the other paddle, snatched at it, had it, stabbed it into the water on the downstream side like Shephard, putting his stomach and shoulders into it, putting everything he ever had into it, digging with the blade for his life.

The boat stopped turning. They were still drifting back, but they were running the edge of an eddy and began angling in, quartering away from what lay below. Adrian did not really think of dying. The certainty of it, should they fail to reach shore, simply registered briefly. He looked only ahead, willing the boat to the side, straining toward a crescent of rocks that broke the flow, forming a quiet pool, a perfect little trout pool. He concentrated on the quiet water, seeing exactly where he would place a dry fly to kiss the edge of current and sweep back to the pool's tail-out. He reached and pulled like a lunging leashed animal, sending the water behind and away with the flat of his paddle.

Suddenly he realized they were closer, far closer than needed for a good cast, and he threw the paddle to the bottom of the boat and clawed for the anchor rock, freeing the stiff line. He stood bent-kneed, coming back with line and rock, pivoting at the waist and hips as he threw.

The coils opened, following the rock, and the anchor fell correctly, well into the pool, just behind the corona of boulders. He hauled slack line, high-elbowed, then came tight, pulling the boat to the anchor, Shepard still digging with his paddle. The bow entered the pool and the stern of the boat swung sweetly behind, coming around wonderfully. Adrian held the line, liking how it felt, still and solid in his hands, wanting to remain forever in this place, this quiet sheltering pool.

Uptik leaped over, water going to his knees. He yanked up the engine's lower unit, said something in a voice that croaked. Shepard dropped his paddle to the bottom of the boat. Billy reached over into the boat, fumbled with a soaked bag, came up with a long-shaft screwdriver. He thrust the blade angrily into the intake opening at the bottom of the jet drive. Adrian looked at his hands still clutching the anchor line, saw the crescent-shaped cut below the big joint of his thumb, the blood oozing thick and bright, feeling nothing, no pain, just a clumsy numbness. He wondered how he had cut himself, but soon was lost again in the incredible wonder of the quiet pool.

"Look," Billy said. He displayed the offending irregularly-shaped stones that had jammed the jet drive. He held them aloft, cursing them, and threw them far out into the river.

At the edges of his meditation on the protecting pool, Adrian became aware of Mike's voice. Finally he understood the words, turned and realized the engine was going again. They were both looking at him. He raised a hand apologetically, and quickly brought in the line and rock, pulling the bow deeper up into the pool as he did so. He gazed sorrowfully to the bottom of his clear pool. Then they were drifting back, but only until Uptik put the engine into gear.

They were still in rapids but the passable breaks in the flow came regularly now, and then the river began to broaden, the banks dropping, and finally the boat moved steadily, and then the river was no longer white. The surface smoothed and quieted, darkening, but still moving powerfully. They came to the forest burn and the place of the huge old, widely scattered boulders that rested like wallowing elephants, and Adrian realized the sound of the engine was now louder than the river. The takeout came a short time later.

Billy angled the stern in, swinging his legs over while a little eddying current slid the boat sideways to the rocky shore.

"Kiss the ground," Mike said, his voice dry.

Back at the cabin, they saw the rods of the other anglers lying in neat rows on the nails in the cabin wall. They placed theirs carefully in the remaining spaces and went inside, into the warmth and glow. There was a card game going. Old Edeas had a neat stack of coins and bills in front of him. He looked exactly like a well-fed coyote.

"Fishin' been good, eh boys?" he said.

"Welcome home," said Jack Ryan. "Get yer waders off and sit in. Somebody's got to help me take some money back from this geezer. How'd you do?"

"Did real well," Adrian told him. He began taking off the stiff, cold boots. Ken Thompson was at his place near the stove.

"How far down river did you go?" he asked.

"Pretty far," Shepard said. "Past the heavy rapids, then down to another, a falls, really, that you wouldn't try to run."

Adrian saw Thompson's eye widen a little.

"You went through those first rapids?"

"All the way," Mike said.

"You fished just above the lip of that falls, then?"

Adrian looked at him. "You wouldn't believe how close," he said.

The other two had stopped their play.

"Well, let's hear it," Ryan demanded. He dug under the table in his mostly empty duffel and brought out what was left of the bottle of single malt. "Give me something to pour in," he told Edeas.

The glasses were on a stand behind him, and Edeas got them.

"We'd like to hear *your* story this time," Ken Thompson looked at them.

Shepard accepted a glass, passed one to Thompson, another to Adrian. "Go ahead," he nodded to Adrian.

"I thought it was bad going down," Adrian began. "That is, the first rapids. But after we saw the wolf, we almost bought it at the pool."

"Wolf, is it?" Ryan broke in. "Now don't skip over the wolf."

"I'll tell you about the wolf," Adrian said.

He told them about the pool, too, and how the anchor had not held, and about the fishing. When he finished that he sipped his drink again, aware of their silence, and remembered how it was just last night listening to Thompson, listening as a total stranger, and he understood that it had changed.

Then he began to tell them about the rapids.

Mr. Bigmouth
Has It Shut Today

After too many days on the road Chris Seres was talking to his dog. Seres and the dog were headed northwest. They had long since left the lovely eastern hill country and were now in a semi-arid scrub landscape that induced a dull torpor. Hot spring sun made water mirages on the highway ahead. They were going downhill now, the first hint of terrain change in the last three hundred miles. At the far end of the false river in the road, Chris registered a splash of bright yellow, focused it into a vehicle parked on the highway shoulder. He eased his foot slightly on the accelerator.

Closer, he made out the figure of a man at the front of the car peering beneath the open hood, emerging suddenly, then slamming the bonnet down with two hands. The man walked

around to the side of the big yellow car, reached in and removed a box, then a long thin object that Seres quickly identi-
fied.

"Fishing rod," he said aloud, having slowed the Fiat considerably by now. The man walked with short determined
steps down the highway, not looking back at his incapacitated
vehicle. Chris saw Asian features, set and resolute as he
passed the fisherman, and pulled off. From his observation
perch the big black dog made a grunting little *uf* of a bark,
turned on its seat perch to face backwards and watch the
hiker come chuffing up.

"Help you with a lift someplace?" Chris said.

The man came to the window, nodded with a quick
formal bow and looked back in disgust at the big yellow
sedan.

"Renter," he said.

"Rental car gave out on you, huh? Well I'm going down
the road if you want a lift."

The man pointed ahead. "Fishing," he indicated.

"I noticed," Chris said. He pointed at the passenger seat
and then down the road. The man nodded, smiled, came
around to the other door and opened it. The wall of black
hairy dog stopped him.

"Here, get back," Chris tugged at the animal. The dog
brought its head back in and smiled happily, its tongue loll-
ing, then struggled to the back. The man came in, pushing his
rod out the sunroof, and placed his tacklebox between his
feet.

Chris introduced himself. The man bowed in the seat,
touched his finger to his chest. "Ito Izawa," he said.

"Glad for the company," Chris said. "This is Dipthong;
Dip, for short," he scratched the big dog. Then he pointed
down the road. "Where you fishing?"

Ito looked at him a moment, then understood. "Fishing," he said, indicating a short distance with his two hands
apart.

Seres nodded. "What you fishing for?"

"Fishing bass," said Ito looking ahead with purpose. He looked at Chris. "You fishing?" he asked.

"You could convince me." Then he caught Ito's real meaning. "Oh, yeah, I fish all right. Fish a lot."

Ito dug in his trouser pocket, removed his wallet and opened it, thumbing through photographs. He found the one he wanted, thrust it at Seres while pointing to himself in the color print. It was a group shot of many anglers, all holding largemouth bass. Ito was located at the center with the biggest fish.

"I number one in bass club. In Japan."

"Hey that's great. Nice fish, too," said Chris. "All nice bass. You must do a lot of fishing."

"Yes. Lot of fishing."

The little Fiat groaned up a long incline, topped the hill crest, and started down. Ahead stretched shoreline marsh and a huge expanse of water on the left. On the right side of the highway, a smaller outlet pond and runoff river lay flat and shining in the sun.

Ito was beginning to speak when the dog caught scent of the water or something else and leaped for the sunroof, its crotch precisely at passenger face level.

"Dipthong, back!" Seres yelled.

The dog slunk down, looking wronged. They turned off the highway into a small flat area where two cars were parked. There was a sign there, informing the interested that the land, the water and marsh as far as one might see, were part of a wildlife refuge. The main lake curved into a bay that ran to the highway and flowed through a culvert under it. At the bay mouth to the main lake was a low brushy point, and Chris saw Canada geese rounding it, heading in. On the bay shore closer to the highway, there was a stocky fellow casting a crankbait. The bay opened onto an arm of what obviously was a reservoir even larger than Seres first suspected. The outlet runoff on the side of the highway where they were parked formed a smallish pond and flowage. An older man and woman were fishing it. The woman sat on an ancient folding chair, a wide-brimmed straw hat pulled down over her forehead, the long canepole in her hands controlling a bright bobber on the quiet water. Her man was headed up the gentle bank. Chris got out of the Fiat and saw that Ito was already across the road tossing the surface plug. The old-timer who'd been fishing the outflow came to the parking area, headed toward his car.

"How's fishin'," Chris asked him.

The fellow shook his head. "Mr. Bigmouf got his mouf shut today," he said. "Got a couple brim."

Chris nodded. He walked down to the main lakeshore. "Catching them?" he called to the stocky angler.

"Not so fast," the man said. "I just got one bass here."

"You use a worm yet?"

"Nope."

"Maybe I'll try that," Chris said. He went back to the car and found a rod and his tacklebox in the mound of luggage. Dipthong wagged his hindquarters happily. "You better stay here, boy. Don't want you messing the fishing." He returned to the main lake.

Ito was a long way around the bay shore now, flailing the water with his surface plug.

"It can be pretty good fishing here sometimes," the stocky angler offered. "Back on the other side, too," he motioned with his head. "I don't know if they got anything or not."

"Guy said a couple of brim," Chris said.

"That don't mean nothin'."

Just then, a small contingent of geese broke off from a larger group and began paddling across the little bay.

"We probably don't need those," the man said. "But I guess they won't stir anything up too bad."

Chris watched the geese, counted five of them before the thought hit him. He was turning toward his car when Dipthong passed him like a cloud shadow racing across the sun. The dog hit the water in perfect retriever form.

"Oh man . . ." the angler began. "That your dog?"

"Yeah."

Chris shouted. Dipthong ignored him. The geese had straightened their necks in alarm and were now paddling for the mouth of the little bay to the main lake. Dipthong's dive took him on a long, gliding angle of interception. One of the Canadas was farther from the others and the dog singled him out, cutting the bird off quite effectively.

Chris reeled in fast, started down the shore shouting for the dog.

"They can't fly yet," the angler told him. "Haven't got their feathers yet. Man I hope the game warden doesn't come."

Dipthong and the goose circled wildly, the dog beginning to gain on the bird. The Canada reared up and beat its wings, gaining a little distance. They went around again.

Three more times the dog closed and each time the goose flapped its way to freedom, but it was plain to see both animals were tiring fast. They neared the place where the stocky angler stood, Dipthong gaining, finally closing and grabbing the bird in a spray of water and flapping wings. They both went under.

Finally, Dipthong surfaced, the goose firmly in his mouth, not struggling, having given itself over to its fate. Dipthong made the bank, dropped the big Canada, and collapsed.

The dog lay on its side, panting, and next to it lay the goose, neck and legs extended full length, breathing as hard as Dipthong. Chris did not approach them, fearing to spur either of them to further exertion.

The goose raised its head. It struggled upright. Finally, it stood unsteadily, observing its foe still prone and heaving for breath, tongue out flat. The goose took two steps, planting a disdainful peck to the dog's side, waddled back to the water and paddled out. The other geese watched silently at the bay mouth. The revived Canada began honking to them.

Chris went to Dipthong, who raised his head. "Take it easy, boy," Seres told him. "You are some kind of foolish." He lifted the dog, carried it back to the car. When he returned, the other angler was fishing a worm."

Chris found his rod on the ground where he had dropped it preparing to dive for the dog and goose.

Out on the point, Ito was casting and retrieving. Chris removed his plastic worm, hooked on a new one.

He walked across the highway and down the bank near the culvert and saw the man and woman were still there. The old gentleman was far down where the pondlike section necked down into a slow-moving river. The woman was closer by having moved her chair near the shore of the widest section of the flowage.

"Howdy," Chris said, being neighborly. "Doin' any good?"

The woman peered up at him from beneath her wide hat brim, nodded and shrugged noncommittedly. Chris walked to where the culvert outflow began to slow and widen. He cast his worm across current, let it sink, then slowly bump along the bottom, swinging 'round into the head of the pond. Then he began to retrieve it, raising his rod tip carefully, dragging the worm, taking up slack, then twitching it lightly using only the rod. He had crawled the lure halfway back when he felt the tap twice, dropped his rod tip and came back hard into the solid resistance of a fish.

"Got 'im. About time," he said aloud, but mainly to himself.

The bass broke surface, went down, then came up in a nice vertical jump, gills flared, head wagging. Chris worked it in through several runs, then lipped it at the water's edge. He hefted it, judged it about three pounds, slipped out the hook and gently dipped it back below the surface. The fish shot away like a watermelon seed squeezed against a marble tabletop. He washed his hand, then rerigged. It took maybe six or seven minutes before the next fish hit.

The bass was a mirror image of the first in size and overall shape. Chris was hunkered down by the water removing the hook when he happened to glance up. The woman had her head raised enough so he could see her face. Her eyes were on him, and they were pleading.

My God, Chris thought. This could be her supper. He lowered the fish into the water, keeping hold of its lower lip.

"Do you want this bass, ma'am?" he asked.

"Yes, I surely would," she answered him. Her voice was dry and slightly raspy.

Chris killed the fish quickly, stood and walked toward her. "Where shall I put it?" he asked.

"Oh, right in this here bucket if you don't mind," she told him.

He saw the white plastic industrial bucket on her far side, in the shade of the chair. There was a damp cloth over its top. He knelt, peeled back the cloth. The high bucket was half full of nice bass. Chris laid his on top of the pile, smiling at himself for having been so easily taken, appreciating the gift of her disclosure. Or maybe it was just fair trade.

"You're not doin' too badly at all," he smiled at her, and saw the bright-toothed, slightly-sheepish grin.

"Not too bad," she told him. "I do appreciate your contribution."

Chris saw the old gentleman approaching them now, and waited until the man had joined them. "I thought Mr. Bigmouth had it shut today," he said.

The old timer's eyes grew round and white. "Well," he said, knowing it was over. "Well . . . you know . . ."

"What you catchin' 'em on?"

"Trickets," said the old fellow. "Trickets and woims."

"I gotcha. You sure are doin' good."

"Yeah. I got to get some bait, heah."

"I'm going to have to tell my friends over there. I promised them. They've got just one fish between them."

The old fellow nodded, fumbling in a plastic cup for his bait.

On the other side of the road, the stocky angler had worked himself out along the curving point. On the far end of the point Ito sat, arms out, elbows on his knees, his head bowed. Chris began walking out.

"What's happening?" he asked.

"Nothin', man. I think your friend gave up, though. I was working my way out there."

"I'll go talk to him."

Ito's rod lay beside him, the plug neatly hooked to one of the guides. The man did not move.

"Hey, Ito, no fish here?"

Ito gazed in depression at the lake. He said nothing for a moment, then looked up in obvious anguish.

"No fish," he said with such sadness Chris thought he might shortly see tears starting down the man's face. Then a puzzled look stole like a shadow across Ito's face. He touched a forefinger delicately to his chest three times. "I number one. Number one bass club man — home."

"Everybody gets skunked sometime," Chris said. "Listen, fish over there. On the other side of the road," he pointed. "I caught two. They caught a bucketful. That man and lady."

There was suddenly a light in Ito's face.

"But they're catchin' them deeper. I got mine on a worm.

You better switch to another bait. Take off that surface plug," he pointed.

Ito frowned. "Topwater," he said. "Only use topwater."

"But those fish are deeper," Chris argued.

"Catch all bass topwater," Ito said stubbornly.

"Don't you have any crankbaits or worms or something?"

Ito shook his head. He pointed to his box. "More topwater."

"Listen, you want to go over to the other side and catch some fish?"

Ito nodded.

"Good let's go. I've got some diving plugs you can use. Will you use my baits? Not topwater."

Ito stood with his rod. "OK," he said.

Chris went to his tacklebox and dug out a medium-running crankbait. He thrust it at Ito.

"Here," he said. "This'll go down. Catch you bass."

Ito took the plug with reluctance.

The woman in the straw hat looked up at Seres. "I see you all came," she said smiling.

"We won't crowd in on your spot," he said.

"That's all right, we done caught a share. But they'll bite all up and down this stretch now."

"That's right," said the old gentleman, who was adding a fish to the bucket. "The way it works here is that when the lake goes up, it starts comin' down through this heah sewah pipe. You get a good flood in this little pond, and current, too, and them ol' basses start feeding."

There was a shout, and they turned to see Ito at the head

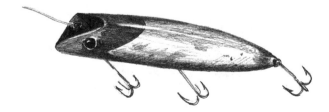

of the little pond, rod bowed, a smile of supreme happiness across his face. He looked at them, giving a thumbs up with one hand, then went back to his fish, talking to it, but not in English. Ito was working his bass shallow to lip it when there was a tortured screeching of brakes followed by a clang of metal door. The truck was circa 1947, and the wizened and scrawny character that emerged from it was as much a relic as his rig. He reached into the rust-eaten, dented bed of the truck, came up with a closed-face reel and ancient gold-finish rod. Then he started down the slope, digging in with the worndown heels of his cowboy boots.

He walked right up to them and you could tell this was his place. "Fishin', huh," he said. The voice was high-pitched, high-decibled. It fit him well. "Y'all shoulda been here this mornin' when it was good. Y'see that little stickup over there. We took thirty-three offun it."

"Thirty-three!" Chris said, disbelieving, and the scrawny type knew it.

"Lemme show yuh." He wound up as though with a baseball bat, and in an incredible parody of a cast, threw the fat-bellied original size Big-O plug at the end of his line in the direction of the stickup. It fell beyond, off the side. The wizened one worked the lure, twitching, yanking, skipping it once out of the water so it somehow began to pass relatively close to the branch. Immediately, the plug was attacked.

"Y'see that!" yelled the newcomer, his great Adam's apple bobbing. "They still be here."

It was as though a switch had been turned on. Now Ito had a strike, missed it, muttering to himself, then struck again and was on. The fellow in the boots was unhooking his fish when the old gentleman and his lady bent their cane-poles simultaneously. They held their fish and soon had them skidding in.

"Ooowee," said the lady from under her hat. "This is how I like it."

Her man got his bass coming, and in one steady, smooth

movement, sailed it through the air to the flat mud shore. "You got to do it like that. You got to be careful not to jerk 'em too bad," he said, looking at Chris. He grinned a broad mouthful of white teeth. "Otherwise, you pull out Mr. Bigmouf's mouf. An' that's not good at all. You get all these little O's lyin around, an' they ain't good for nothin'."

Chris was laughing. It was total madcap. Up and down the shore bass were being hooked, coming off, sailing in, accompanied by the shouts of the anglers. He finally remembered the rod in his own hand, made several casts, and took a fish. Ito was riveted to his productive spot plainly unmovable for the duration. He looked at his watch. He was overdue. He walked up to Ito.

"I got to go," he said. "I know you don't want to ride back to your car right now."

Ito's total attention was fixed on the water. Finally what Seres was telling him registered. He turned, looked at Chris, looked up the bank to the Fiat. Dipthong stood half through the sunroof watching them, no doubt ready to share his space with a rider.

"Fish," said Ito. "Many fish. I get other ride. OK?"
Then he looked worried. "You want plug back?"
Chris laughed. "No, you keep it."
Ito smiled thankfully. "So many fish!"

"You catch them," Seres said. He collected his box, waved to the old gent and his old lady. "Thanks," he said. "Have a good supper."

The couple smiled at him.

"You missin' out," the old gentleman said. "Mr. Bigmouf, he don't always have it 'shut' like dis."

"That's a good thing," Chris said. "There'd be nothing left."

He climbed up the bank, walked back to his car. Inside Dipthong greeted him with a small *uf* and tried to crawl into his lap. He got the dog back to his perch and started down the road.

Torrents

Almost there, almost at camp, Nick Stroud pulled in at the small bar and restaurant named for the great Canadian river, the river he had wanted to fish for over twenty years. His guide was already there.

With two green beer bottles between them on a good table looking out at the small town, Stroud drowned the dryness of the long trip in three swallows. He eyed his guide, Fred Buller, a big fellow in a dark waxed cotton sport cap, then placed his glass on the bare table.

"Tell me up front, Fred," he said. "Has it been too hot, or should I have been here last week?"

"Can you cast?" Buller asked.

Stroud smiled. "I've fished salmon a good bit."

"I never guarantee fish. Especially I don't guarantee a salmon. If you can cast for me, I'm going to guarantee you a salmon."

Stroud leaned forward. "Has it been that good?"

"I had a man and woman yesterday who'd never fished for any but little things down in the States. They couldn't even cast. They had five fish on. Lost them of course." Now he leaned conspiratorially close. "The river's full of fish. They're *averaging* twenty pounds!"

They finished their drinks, went out, Stroud ticking off a mental list of things that could go wrong the next day. If they did, there would surely be the opportunity to try again. He had the contacts now to get on the river, and his software rep business was doing well enough that he could call his time away. At forty-nine you ought to start doing a few things for yourself. And so he did not knock the age of the computer, though personally he couldn't stand the things.

They took their respective vehicles, Stroud in the turbo-charged Saab, Buller in an old gray Dodge pickup, and headed only a short way up river, Buller leading, before pulling into a turnoff that went down to the water. They were only a short way from the saltwater bay into which the river emptied.

"Let's just stand here a bit," Buller said. "Do you know how to get to the Doctor's camp?"

"It's just up ahead and off this road, isn't it? He drew me a map — it's in the car."

The breeze had been steady, but now a gust of wind came up the river and hit them. Stroud's graying blond hair whipped before his eyes for a moment, and Buller tugged down his dark cap.

"You just take the first gravel road past the fourth intersection," Buller said. "You know it's on the first pool up from saltwater."

"Yes. It was awfully good of him to let me use it. I'm sorry he had to cancel out, though."

They watched the big river moving steadily to its meeting with the sea, and they both saw the fish simultaneously. Two big salmon cleared the water in curving leaps that took

them well forward, no real reason for them to jump like that, no rapids here, the jumping simply an explosive release — a purging of a fraction of the enormous energy they now possessed fresh from the sea. Soon another then a fourth fish broke, all of them obviously moving upstream, not the nearly straight up bursts of fish holding in a pool.

"Aerialized torpedoes," Stroud said. "They're thick!"

"Yes," Buller agreed.

"And you're right; they're big."

Buller just nodded, smiling.

"How long have they been showing like this?" Nick Stroud asked.

"This is the second day."

Then Stroud killed the guide's pleasant musing.

"How bad's your poaching?" he asked.

"Not good. But we're keeping them off balance on the river. A run like this, though, they'll hit it at the mouth, in the bay."

"And they haven't yet?"

"No. Already a lot of fish in the first two pools though. We'll be all right, even if . . ."

A late model U.S. sedan pulled smoothly into the turnoff above the river where they had parked. They looked up and Stroud was surprised to see the tall elderly gentleman climbing from the vehicle.

"That looks like . . ." he began.

"It is," Buller interjected. "He's been here four days, now. Planning a three-week stay. He's looking for a grander. I think he's feeling at his age, well . . ."

The white-haired gentleman walked up to them just then, and the three exchanged greetings but soon turned back to watch the river. More fish showed themselves, always moving up current.

"Look there," the elder angler pointed, his arm suddenly cutting the air to the right where the river's surface closed over the back of a rolling fish. "Did you see it?"

Stroud and Buller had not.

"It was one of the big ones."

"Bigger than those jumpers? They had to be eighteen to maybe over twenty pounds," Stroud said.

"Yes, quite a bit heavier."

"Fred said you were looking for an especially big fish."

The older man smiled. In his lifetime he had taken salmon in sizes and in places that were vague dreams for most anglers. Salmon were his passion. His life. "I don't know how much longer I'm going to be able to do this — or be around, for that matter," he said, pleasantly. "Yes, I'd like one more big fish. Maybe the biggest fish." He paused.

They were all looking at the right place when the big salmon broke again, this time lifting completely from the water, then slamming the surface heavily as it fell back. There was a brief wake caused by its forward progress.

"Yes, I'd like one like that one," the man nodded. "Forty pounds of fish, I'd think."

He wished them luck then, expected to see them on the river, and then he left.

Of course they spoke of him for awhile. And then it was time to go.

"My boat's already down at the first pool," Buller said. "The first pool will be the one now."

"Unless they stop them coming in tonight," said Stroud. "Who's your fish warden these days?"

"Jim Clarke, for the district. Good man. Some from the other districts aren't, I'm afraid. Get bribed off, decoyed off or scared off. Jim's had his share of threats, but he keeps on going. They assign assistants to the wardens now — always one of the Indians. Usually he ends up being a relative of one of the biggest poachers. I won't kid you. You're right about a run like this. There's too much money at stake for them to let it go."

"Well, nothing much we can do," Stroud said.

"You can bet Jim won't be getting much sleep for awhile now. We can count that on our side."

They drove the road to the Doctor's camp, and before they reached it, Buller stopped to show Stroud where his boat was pulled ashore at the end of a footpath to the river.

"Come by for coffee first, if you like," Stroud told him.

"Fine," the guide said. "Get some good sleep."

There was a strong rapids at the head of the first great pool from the bay. Above it, halfway up the wooded shore that formed the long holding water of the second pool, the warden, Jim Clarke, stood with his assistant watching the water.

"Two fish," Clarke said, not pointing, knowing his man, Vincent Cain, had seen them as well.

"But not so many like down below," the short, stocky, young assistant said.

"No, they'll probably leave this alone — 'til later," Clarke said. He was barely taller than his assistant, sturdily built, a man of middle age with dark hair beginning to gray. "There's gas enough in the boat?"

"Yep." Cain looked at the sky, turned downriver toward the breeze that was marked by more heavy gusts than before. "Maybe weather comin'," he said.

"Probably right. We won't have to worry about the boat if it blows enough. They'll hit the first pool for sure if they can't work the mouth."

Cain grunted, nodded once.

"Better plan for all night," Clarke said. "I don't know why they didn't try to hit it last night."

"Maybe waitin' for more fish inside," Cain said. "Maybe no fish holding near the mouth — just comin' right up the river."

"Could be." Clarke eyed the assistant quickly. The man had been consistently correct in his evaluation of the actions of the poachers. Accuracy, Clarke expected, that probably came from past first-hand experience. As long as it was history, that was fine. Nothing better than a reformed poacher who knew the tricks. But you could never be certain that tribal or distant family relationships weren't still more important. It was some balancing trick these men played, and Clarke was fairly sure that it ended up a split commitment. One for them, one for law enforcement. But he had not yet been working with Cain when he thought the stolid little man had tried to foul an arrest.

"What time you want to meet?" asked Cain.

"About ten. If they start it'll be a lot later."

"You bringin' some dinner?"

"I could."

"All night, you get pretty hungry."

"I'll bring some coffee, too," Clarke said.

Nick Stroud racked his cleaned dinner dish, walked to his tackle bag by the window on the far side of the camp's main room. It was too dark now for him see the river. The window was open. The gusts of wind were keeping down the usual horde of insects beating themselves against the screening, trying to reach the Coleman lanterns burning inside.

Stroud slung the tackle bag to a table, sat down and began removing his reels. A bottle of his favorite single malt Scots whiskey stood on the eating table. He had not taken a drink before dinner, nor had he poured one now. There was not going to be even the slightest hint of a headache in the morning. This river and all it stood for had lived with him so long, he wanted it perfect this first time. The run of truly big salmon for which the river was known had come, was coming each hour, and for once he had the luck to be there, and he was going to be the best he could. He stripped the lines from each reel in turn, checking first the line-to-backing connection, then the line-to-leader butt junction. He looped on fresh leaders, testing each connection, looking for nicks or any weaknesses in the monofilament leaders. He mounted the reels on rods, put leader envelopes and clippers away, his excitement building all the while. Pegs that served as rod racks were nailed to the camp wall beneath the porch roof. While he was placing his rigged rods across them, the first slashes of jagged lightning exploded across the sky far to the south. Stroud muttered a quiet oath.

"What can you do, though," he said aloud. "All right, if it's got to storm, let it come now and get it over."

He went in, eyeing the bottle wistfully before going to bed.

The storm came. It descended in sudden violence. The wind buffeted the camp, waking him. And then the rain came. It roared in on a second wall of wind, solid sheets blowing and beating along the river, cascading from the building's roof in solid falls.

Stroud could not sleep. *Why me?* he wondered in the night. *Why this time?* When the rain subsided, he thought he could hear a thundering sound from the south and thought it would have to be a surf of angry waves built by the wind where the river met the great saltwater bay. Then the rain came hard again, and the thundering was mainly a deep sensation in the back of his head. Stroud thrashed in his bed in frustration. When at last he slept it was still raining.

Through the last wooded stand near the mouth of the river, a rutted track ran down almost to shore. A rust-eaten and filthy pickup had pushed as far as possible to the end of the track, using no lights, one of four men in the truck walking ahead, looking for hazards. The driver stopped, killed the engine. He, the other man in the cab and another in the truck bed got out. The driver was a giant of a man, not merely in height, but in bulk, and with the seat of the full-size truck in its extended position, he had to squeeze himself to clear the steering wheel. In darkness, they moved through the brush to the river bank.

The smell of the sea was strong on the wind coming from the bay and the huge gulf beyond. Surf at the river mouth thundered heavily over the hiss of rain.

"No way we're going to get the boat out there," said the man who had walked ahead of the truck.

"Gotta be the first pool," said the huge man.

"Warden's going to be there," one of the other's said.

"Too bad. You know how much we lose if we miss this?" the big man said. "Hell, that Clarke — he been lucky too long anyway." He was silent a moment. "We got a boat all ready for us up there. That Buller's boat. Tied all nice and waitin'."

"He got a sport to fish, must be." One of them said. "How'd you know?"

The big man grinned invisibly in the dark, and rain washed his cheeks and ran from his thin, ragged moustache onto his bared teeth. "I know all right," he said.

"Well let's go then," someone said.

They turned and climbed the bank back to the truck. The driver's size permitted only one passenger in the cab of the truck. The man who had walked the track earlier climbed into the bed with one of the others. They lay on an ancient tarp covering a snarl of monofilament gill net that stank of rotting fish and slid in the dirt and grit on the bottom of the bed. The truck backed to a turnaround and bounced up the track to another road.

Warden Jim Clarke rumpled his son's curly hair a last time, left the boy's bedroom and walked to the coat rack by the kitchen. He took his dark rain jacket, slipped into it, then came back to his wife standing by the fireplace. The blonde woman was much younger than Clarke.

"I'm glad you were home to see Ian," she told him. "He misses you the next day after these all-nighters."

"Wish I didn't have to sleep, Meg," he said. "Wish we'd get this mess stopped."

She handed him the sandwiches and a vacuum bottle of coffee, tilted her face up to be kissed. And then he left.

The rain hit him hard, and he yanked the slicker closed, heading to his truck. He turned the defroster on full after starting the engine, jammed into first gear and started for the place he had agreed to meet Cain.

The four poachers moved surely in darkness. The big man and one of the others had found Fred Buller's boat without trouble. They emptied tackle from it, tossing an expensive rod to the ground while the other two brought down the long gill net. The rain had lessened but already the water level of the river was rising quickly. Two of the poachers slipped the boat into the river, dropped and started the outboard.

They were at the closest holding water below the rapids at the head of the first pool. The boat pushed into the current, streaming the net's long lead line. The big man held it wrapped once around his upper arm instead of tying it off. The men in the boat began putting out the net, letting the weights unfurl the meshes as they slowly dropped down current. They stretched the net full; then, using their comrade as an anchor point, commenced a long curving sweep back to shore.

The boat was only halfway in when the big man felt them, felt the throbbing life in the net, its weight increasing so suddenly that despite his size he stumbled forward into the river, sloshing water into his boots until he caught his balance. The other man, who remained ashore, helped pull the lead line, and then the boat was in the shallows again, the two poachers in it leaping out, all of them manhandling the net, ripping it in fiercely.

The net bulged, throbbed, a living thing that jolted them as they dragged it in. One of the poachers who had been in the boat and the smaller man who had remained ashore wore headlamps with red lens coverings. They turned them on now, and the pale beams flickered over the long, powerful forms of the trapped Atlantic salmon. In one writhing mass the fish attempted escape, mouths agape, teeth or gills caught in the meshes, eyes staring, bodies and tails lashing violently.

The men leaped upon them with lead-weighted clubs, smashing at them in the net, grabbing individual fish that had thrashed loose and, before they could escape, clubbing them in the shallows, kicking or throwing them to the bank where one of poachers waited to beat them to death. The man on the shore stuffed the dead or nearly dead salmon into huge sacks.

Here and there the poachers' ancient, rotted net had breaks in the meshes, and at these points, a fish might find its way to freedom that would often be short lived. The cutting monofilament would have done too much damage to the gill rakers, and the fish would live a brief time before dying, never having spawned. But most of the fish that found temporary freedom at the net breaks were intercepted by the poachers. Cursing, they descended upon the great salmon, grabbing tails, gills, or simply cupping bellies, heaving the fish toward the shore.

They were big fish, few under twenty pounds, many far larger, the prime breeding stock of their species, irreplaceable living gene pools of the race, headed for smokehouses, restaurants, and black marketeers. A huge fish had found the tear in one of the meshes, and began writhing through. The big poacher saw it and with a guttural sound thrashed forward, over his boots, club coming down, hitting water and the back of the fish as it slipped out and away into the river. The big man shook himself in rage, sloshing back. The net was empty.

They stood a moment, breathing hard, soaked with rain, fish gore spattered over their shirt fronts and boots, slime running from fingers that hung curled at their sides, blood showing dark in the illumination of the head lamps.

"Douse them lights, now!" the big man ordered. "Get out again with that net. Gonna clean 'em up tonight. You know how much we gonna make tonight?" He laughed in childish delight.

They floated the sacks of fish in the shallows downstream to the place where they would commence the next swing with the net. Near the tail of the pool where they would make the final netting effort, their truck waited. Now the big poacher and the man helping him dragged the sacks up the shore so they would not float away. Again they fed line as the boat pulled out, disappearing in darkness, spreading, stretching the deadly net. The river was broader here with deep holding pockets. Two low rocky islands lay mid-stream, slicing the current, and the boatmen headed for the larger of them. The level of the river was rising steadily now, the current strengthening.

They made their circle from the near shore of the island, and as they began curving back the pull and weight of the net became too strong for the two men ashore. Quickly they threw a wrap of the line over a boulder, not knowing if the increased resistance was current or what was struggling below in the net. The boat materialized again, slipping smoothly into the shallows, and as the net rose, they could see its surfacing edge gleaming, humping darkly from the bodies of the trapped fish. The boatmen were out, clawing at the net, when the high-intensity light hit them, the shock of it physically jarring them. Jim Clarke's voice slapped at them a second later.

"Stop it there, don't pull it any farther," the warden ordered.

The moment the white light hit them, the big poacher leaped up slope into the bordering woods. The other three remained transfixed.

"Come on out of there, Francois," Clarke ordered. "Nobody else the size of you lives in this country. Don't need a light to identify you. Now get!"

Watching the poachers in the glare of his light, he turned slightly, calling in a quieter voice to his assistant. "Bring him out of there, Vincent," he directed.

The big man came, but not from the direction or the way in which Clarke expected. He loomed up behind and on the warden's off side, stepping quickly for his huge bulk, swinging a short pinwheeling blow from his hip that cracked Clarke on the back of the head behind his left ear.

"You remember good how big Francois is," he growled. "You remember to forget all 'bout him."

The warden stumbled forward, knees buckling, still conscious, trying for balance. Francois moved in quickly now, hooking with his left, the huge fist smashing Clarke in the side of the head and upper jaw. It was a stunning blow that initially left numbness and the crumbling sensation of gravel in his mouth that, as he dropped, Clarke knew was the ruin of his teeth on that side. The certainty that his jaw was broken registered in a detached way as he fell to the stone beach. A sea of redness swelled before him as he slammed into the ground. Still conscious, clawing to stay that way, he curled fetally as Kahn started at him with his feet, kicking.

The other three poachers came in unopposed, the warden's assistant gone in the night. The smallest poacher rolled the warden over, hefted him half-way to his feet, allowing Francois to get at his underside. The huge man pummeled Clarke unmercifully, then hammered a final jackhammer blow straight in the man's face.

Francois stepped back, rubbing the cut flesh of his fists, looked around, a maddened creature, then grabbed the unconscious warden by the back of his collar, dragged him to the boat, and dumped him in. He ordered one of the netters to the outboard, and they started out into the river.

The big man took out a folding knife, sawed at the anchor line and cut it easily. He waved the man on the tiller ahead, motioning toward the island. The boat ground ashore and Francois vaulted out with the anchor line, grabbing Clarke, hauling him through the shallow water and up the low beach. The other poacher followed him.

"What you doing?" the smaller man said.

"Helpin' him remember."

Francois dragged the warden to a nest of four boulders not far up the beach. The boulders were on a point that thrust directly upriver, slicing the current. He pulled Clarke back to the boulder nearest the water and began binding the unconscious man with the anchor line.

"Water come up, maybe he drown," said the smaller poacher.

"Maybe dead already," Francois said. "Think maybe his face caved in. If he ain't, and he don't drown, then he gonna remember good."

"He got a little kid."

"Yeah, we got kids, too, gotta feed."

Francois yanked his final knot tight, dropped the line, looked down at the unconscious man and spit at his legs. They moved quickly back to the boat.

Incredibly, the four went back to work. When they finished seining all the holding water of the pool that the increased current and rising water permitted, they had reached their takeout. Francois spoke to one of the men who worked the net.

"Take this Buller's boat back up where it's safe. Where it was," the big man ordered. "He makes his livin' on the river."

There was no sun, and the river ran dark and heavy in the morning when Stroud and Buller made their way toward the place where the guide had secreted his boat. They broke through the last of the high willow and alders, and Buller stopped.

"Trouble," the guide said.

Stroud knew it was more than the night's rain and the river, and followed where Buller pointed.

"I tied the boat here. Anchor line's gone. So's my rod."

He stepped carefully around the area, found the rod and reel, the rod's tip section broken. "They've worked the pool."

"Poachers," Stroud said flatly.

Buller nodded, looking out over the heavy river.

"No sense in even bothering, then, with that and the water, both," said Stroud.

"I don't have much hope," Buller said. "But the way the fish were coming — there were so many in the run that more could have moved in after the net. We're on the moon, though you couldn't have seen it last night. And there's no way they could have worked the mouth in the bay in that weather. That's why they moved in here." He fingered the broken rod, placed it gently in the boat. "Do you have a sinking line?"

"Yes."

"We fish the heavy spring water about like this. Anchor and send big streamers down. They left the extra anchor line

I have under my seat. I could make a rock anchor. It's up to you."

"Maybe they netted all the fish," Stroud said.

"All they could," Buller answered. "They couldn't stop fresh ones from coming in, though."

"What do they get for them, black market?"

"At least four-and-a-half-dollars. You're talking ninety for a twenty-pound fish. There were a lot of much bigger fish in here. Much bigger. Round it off to a hundred a fish — and that's conservative — and figure they got a hundred salmon in this stretch. That wouldn't be hard. That's ten thousand dollars for the night's work."

They ran the edge of the main current, heading down, Stroud looking for a change in water that would indicate the lies. The guide slowed, checked their forward progress with the engine, then twisted open the throttle, cursing, heading directly for the gravel point.

Stroud jerked his head up, looked ahead, back at the guide, then at the island again.

"Those stinking, vicious . . ." Buller began cursing, and did not stop.

The boat sliced ahead at speed helped by the current. Stroud grabbed the gunwales, bracing, stared ahead, saw it then, saw the crumpled human figure bound to the rocks.

Buller cut the throttle back, kicked into reverse to keep them from splintering on the point. The big river canoe ground on the gravel and Stroud barely kept himself from slamming into the bow brace. They were both out instantly, running toward the bound man, his legs in water halfway up his thighs.

Buller's knife, shining silver in the dull light, came up through the first of the bonds, cutting cleanly with one quick sawing movement. "Good, God," he panted. "To do this . . ."

A hopeless moan escaped from the battered warden. Both his eyes were swollen shut. His broken nose bent horribly to the side, the lips purple, split, engorged. A small trickle of blood ran from his mouth as they lifted him, carried him to the boat.

"Easy Jim, easy now, lad," Buller almost crooned to the man.

They gentled him into the boat, putting cushions beneath his head. Buller pulled the boat from the point, ripped the engine alive, and headed down river for the camp where Stroud was staying.

After the hospital, the call to the beaten warden's wife, Stroud and Buller stood at the access near the rivermouth. The surf was down, but long rollers still broke occasionally, showing white in the bay, and the river ran high and ugly, bringing its load of flotsam to the sea.

"He'll never be the same," Buller said. "I don't mean physically. The jaw and nose will set. They'll probably have to get a new man now. Look," he turned to Stroud, "why don't you get a rest. I'll come back later in the afternoon and we can talk about what to do."

"Fine," Stroud told him. He dug in his vest and brought out a battered flask, unscrewed the top, offering it.

Buller nodded. "I'll break the rule today," he said, accepting the drink.

Driving up the main road before the turnoff to the camp, Buller slowed for the oncoming vehicle. The elderly angler whom they had met the day before extended his arm from his window, palm toward them. They stopped, parallel to one another.

Will you be able to stay a few days?" the man asked, looking up at Stroud. "It's virtually unfishable, as you obviously know. It would be a shame. The salmon are here."

"I'm afraid only one more day," Stroud said. "Have you tried at all?"

"Not today. Did I mentioned to you yesterday — I've taken several good fish from this run — before the rain." He smiled thinly. "Not the grander, though. It could go down enough by tomorrow midday. It might be fine for you." He looked at Buller. "I heard about the warden."

Buller nodded. "Awful thing."

"It didn't take long for the word to get out," said Stroud.

"It's all they're talking about in town," said the angler. "I heard it at breakfast. How will he take it?"

"If I had a wife and kid, I don't know what I'd do," Buller said. "Jim may very well hang them. And then he'll probably move."

They looked up to see several vehicles waiting behind them in the road.

"Good luck," the grand old angler waved to Stroud.

Late in the afternoon, Stroud slowly woke from exhausted sleep, drawn slowly to consciousness by the piercing, incessant sound outside the cabin. He could not at first identify it, then realized it was the gulls. He rose, sloshed water in his face, staggered for his trousers, then slipped on knee-high rubber boots without socks. He walked out onto the porch.

Gulls circled overhead, over the beach, hunting. He could make out more of the birds on the stony shore below, working at something. He walked down three steps from the porch, started down the trail to the river. He heard the sound of a vehicle coming, looked at his watch as he continued, thinking it should be the guide.

Walking faster now, he saw the humped form at water's edge, realizing what it was. The gulls around it flapped screeching at his approach. He slowed just a moment, sucking in his breath, then moved quickly to the carcass of the dead salmon. He bent down, not believing it's size.

The fish was only slightly bloated. The gulls had taken its eyes, but the hugeness of it was what mattered. Stroud shook his head, then grasped the wrist ahead of the tail and moved the great fish higher on the beach. He started back up, seeing Buller coming.

"There's a fish, a dead salmon," Stroud called. "Do you have a scale?"

Buller raised his hand, nodding. He returned with a good brass hand scale, and they walked to the fish.

Buller knelt beside it. "This is what they took," he said. "The breeders like this. You see this?" His hand traced the brutal net marks on the flanks of the great fish.

"Yes," Stroud told him.

"It broke free. Probably last night. Maybe not. Doesn't matter. It's dead and never spawned."

He slipped the scale hook beneath a gill cover and lifted the carcass. Stroud read the scale.

"Forty . . . forty-seven-and-a-half pounds!" Stroud said. Buller lowered the dead fish to the beach.

"My God, that was the . . . that was *his* fish!" Stroud said softly.

"Maybe it would have been yours," Buller said. "This is what's in the river. You're at least young enough to try a lot longer."

Stroud looked at him and at the salmon and the river. "Maybe," he said. "Maybe age doesn't have anything to do with it. Maybe the clock's about run out."

Together they slipped the remains of the great salmon into the river. The current caught it quickly, turning it once, taking it out.

First Tarpon

W e crossed from the islands in the small plane, watching the sun melt and spread as it touched the curved horizon. It was some time before the smokey vermilion glow of its passing was gone. When we landed it was dark, and we were hungry. We picked up our rental cars and headed down the highway, looking for a place to eat. A little pasta house looked inviting. Like fighter pilots in formation, we broke from the highway and angled our cars into the parking lot. Inside, it was low-lit with a single wall lamp in each red-padded booth. Quiet enough for talking.

"Good trip," I said settling.

"Both weather and fish," Adam Garret said. "I learned a lot about bonefish."

"You don't get to do too much of it?"

"I will. More tarpon, though."

We had just met at the camp, and fished from separate boats while there.

"I've really just been fishing for tarpon a short time, though," Adam added. "Trying to play catchup." He was a tall, dark, intense young man, and at this time, totally immersed in the world of angling.

"How'd you get started?" I asked. Some of the more fascinating stories revolve around why people start fishing. There are a lot of reasons. Adam's stopped me cold.

"I broke my back," he said. "Going over the hurdles in steeplechase. You get a lot of thinking done in three months hanging from a hospital ceiling. I knew when I got out of there I still wanted a sport that could become a passion, but one that didn't require a precise number of players like squash or polo — I played those, too. But *fishing*! The only interest I ever had in it was my grandfather's tackle. I liked the look of it. I used to play with it. Sometimes he took me to the old Abercrombie and Fitch in New York. It was like an amusement park for a kid.

"When I was walking again, a friend took me fishing in the Catskills. I brought my grandfather's old yellow bamboo rod. We didn't catch much. But we had fun — so much fun. That was the start of it. I can't stop, now."

"That's bad?" I said.

Adam laughed. "No. It was trout first, of course, then salmon and steelhead and then I started this saltwater fly fishing, which is totally fascinating. There's so much involved. I keep dreaming some day I'll be able to cast a whole flyline — into the wind!"

"I saw you out there. You don't do too badly right now."

"Not yet," he said deprecatingly. "Some day. But I certainly jumped into this saltwater game at the top. I'd been reading about it — everything I could get my hands on. But what I'd actually been doing physically before coming down

here to the Keys for the first time was fishing Trico imita-
tions — numbers twenty-two and twenty-eight — on a rod like
a feather, casting maybe thirty feet! Then I tried *this*."

"That must have been some kind of shock."

"Oh yes. But the same kind of intensity. I did all kinds of
research trying to find the guide I thought would be right for
me. I had the gall to presume I might find the Senator free
and that he'd fish me. He was booked, but he suggested five
names, five guides, and one of them — Dana Williams — was a
young man who was just getting started full time. He'd been
a commercial fisherman farther north, and was said to be
trying a little harder, trying to build his book of clients, and
he agreed to take me.

"We began earlier than usual for here; around seven in
the morning. The weather was wrong, the water really too
cool. Dana poled me all day and at the end of the day we saw
one bonefish at a hundred and fifteen feet, going away, and he
wanted me to cast! And there it was. It was late, too. He'd
stayed out when everyone else was gone or going in — about
five or five-thirty — and after that bonefish he was as disap-
pointed as I was. Then he said, 'Look, do you want to try for a
shot at a tarpon?' And I said sure. He told me it was very
much an off chance. It was really too early, the water was still
too cool, but we'd try. We went over to the ocean side, and
they were there."

The waitress came then, and we were both into his story
enough that the ordering was a sketchy thing. Some ver-
micelli, clam sauce . . .

"There was this little channel we came into, going with
the tide, and they were moving toward us like slow, dark
torpedos so there was no need for a long cast. I got the fly out,
got it started back, and a fish came for it, and Dana was
yelling 'he's coming, he's coming, he's taking . . . strike, for
God's sake!' I couldn't see the fish, but I struck anyway. He
was there. He was there just for an instant, because he or
something cut the shock tippet — the eighty-pound stuff —

just like that. But he had been there. I felt what it was like for a moment, and I knew what it was going to really be like then. I didn't think I was ready for it.

"Then in a little pocket outside the channel we saw a huge fish lying up. I couldn't even shoot line yet. I had an old glass rod for a thirteen line, and I was pumping, pumping just to get fifty-five feet out, and Dana was trying to get us closer but not spook the fish. Somehow I pumped a sixty-foot cast out. I saw him move over toward the fly and I stripped it once, and he took that fly. And then it started."

I sipped my wine. Adam clutched a tall glass of water, the ice rapidly melting, condensation running down the outside of his glass.

"The tarpon jumped right away and kept going, jumping all the way. I had some old antireverse reel and never knew when I was gaining line. I just cranked. Somewhere along during all those hours I finally learned to pump."

"All those hours?"

Adam drank some of his ice water. "I was on that fish essentially eight hours. Seven hours, fifty-two minutes to be exact."

"My God!"

"I learned something else. Maybe twenty jumps later I learned I could tell when he was coming up. I could feel him shaking his head and body, those tail beats getting stronger when he was starting up. Before it was over he jumped thirty-seven times, by Dana's count."

"Eight hours," I said, knowing what that would do to a man, remembering a friend's ten hour fight.

"But I was so high. It never really got to me — until later."

The food came. We picked at it a little.

"In the beginning, Dana used the engine," Adam continued. "He motored slowly after the fish, trying to keep our distance to it down — especially when the fish was green. But remember, we had fished all day and didn't have much gas left. The tarpon moved into deeper water. We tried to hold him back, hold him shallow, but it was no good. Then we ran out of gas. It was far too deep to pole. 'Now he'll have to tow the boat,' Dana said.

"Three hours into the fight the bull shark came. He stayed near us a little while, then slowly headed for the tarpon. And he was big. Awfully big. Dana allowed as how we ought to think about breaking off the fish, and I allowed as how we ought to think about a way to frighten off the shark. The tarpon did it for us.

"After all that time, hooked like he was, he ran for the shark, and he drove it off. But the shark still stayed with us for a long time after that. I remember it looking very dark and big in the water.

"Someone had called Dana earlier on the radio, worried because he wasn't in. Now different captains called us from time to time to ask if we were still on. Maybe he felt responsible because he'd put Dana and me together, but the Senator himself came on the radio. He tried to talk me through the fight, or at least help me begin turning it our way. It was awfully good of him. My backing was way out there. It kept collecting little pieces of grass, increasing the drag, and Dana leaned out over the water unbelievably far picking them off, not touching anything but the little pieces of grass. Then I tried to change the angle of pull, to get the fish coming, and he did move. He circled. He started slowly, then angled back so fast, so sharply it was faster than I could pick up line. The slack bowed back, and we were still too deep so Dana couldn't turn the boat with the pole. What happened was, the slack line became tangled around the engine.

"We worked on it and finally he took my rod to pass under the engine, then gave it back. 'Now all hope for a record is over,' Dana told me. 'I touched your rod.' Record? I didn't give a damn about any record. I only cared about the fish. I just wanted the fish. God, I wanted the fish.

"Then I began to get the tarpon coming. I couldn't believe he would ever tire. I thought we would just go on like that forever, maybe until one of us died. Then he began to turn from my pressure. But I didn't know about fishing such a fish. He came to the surface sliding slowly, slowly, toward me through the water, but then he would roll on his side and take air into his false lung and turn that eye, that great eye on me and just — go away again. Dana told me when he got air like that it would replenish him. He didn't tell me what to do about it. I didn't know what to do. What the hell was I supposed to do? You know, I was the trout specialist who mastered ten- and twelve-inch brook trout in those little tiered mountain streams! The tarpon came like that again. It happened several times. I don't remember how many. But he would come and look at me, rolling to take his air, and go away. Then all of a sudden it was dark.

"It was dusk one minute, and then it was — black. It was awesome. It was frightening. You didn't know what was out there. Anything could be. Anything probably was. Still, when he hadn't done it for awhile, Dana would come to the bow and kneel ahead of me on the platform where I stood. He'd hook a foot under the foredeck and lean out there into the

darkness feeling for the weed on my backing and take it off, for as far as he could reach. I began to fear he would fall in. For almost eight hours I lived in total fear that I'd lose the fish.

"The tarpon towed us in the dark but he was slower now, much slower. But he was still moving. I tried not to think about the strain on the fifteen-pound tippet all this time — the strain on the knots, the kind of purchase the hook still had in the fish's mouth. I had no idea where we were or how far we had come, but it was plenty of miles, Dana said. I could see lights to the west but they weren't close enough and strong enough to overpower the brightness from the moon and the stars. When we would be in line with the moon, the water lit up — a long bright ripply path going off into the darkness. It worried me that I started noticing that because it meant I was beginning to lose my concentration on the fish. Every time the fish seemed to slow, I tried him, tried to turn his head, and around one o'clock that morning he started coming for good.

"I brought him in several times. Each time he came just so close to the boat, then slid on past the way they do, just outside reach, and circled out a little more line again. Then on one pass he let me bring him closer, close enough. He was at the boat, all silvery in the moonlight, still swimming, so weakly, but still swimming. Eight hours, and he was still swimming, and I knew I hadn't really hurt him. I had tired him terribly, the way he had me, but I hadn't mortally hurt him.

"Dana said I had to have this fish after all this, after everything. He could reach the tarpon with the big, long-handled gaff, the killer gaff. He could reach and get him. The rod was bent all the way over, and I was holding him completely, and I couldn't kill this fish. Dana said 'All right, we'll try to get him with the release gaff. This is where we lose him if we're going to lose him,' and it was out of him before I could tell him anything about not putting his mouth on the fish like that.

"I had the rod bent so that I feared it would break and if it did, the force from being released from all that pressure would snap it back into Dana's face or hit him in the side of the head, but he said not to worry. He was over the gunwale, reaching, telling me to lift so he could get the short release gaff hook in the tarpon's mouth when he grabbed the leader. I had the rod bent double trying to lift that fish, and he was coming. His head was rising in the moonlight, and I could see the fly in the corner of his mouth, the hook shiny in the moonlight, and his mouth as wide and black as all the night, and when the tippet broke the rod didn't go whipping back to hit Dana, it just straightened about to the horizontal.

"I know what dying is like. Dying is easy. Dying is like that. It is simply anticlimax. And then we had to radio to another guide to bring us gas so we could get back. I was overdue back home so I drove crazy to the airport. I missed my plane anyway. Then I called my girlfriend, and I called my father. I talked to them trying to tell them, but they couldn't understand what it was like, what it meant.

"I didn't know what to do, then, so I went back to my rental car and slept a couple of hours there and then the next plane took me home. I got home and I collapsed. My arm and hand began to hurt, then cramp in my sleep and out of my sleep. I fought that fish for a week in my sleep. I dreamed the tarpon god had sucked out my brain. Nothing, no other fishing has it like that. And that was my first tarpon."

Adam leaned back against the padded cushioning of the booth. I pushed away the little-eaten food.

"What time is it?" he asked.

I looked at my watch and told him.

"My God, I'm going to miss my plane! I've got to go . . ."

With a quick "good-bye," he dashed out of the restaurant. Tires screeched for an instant. He waved, grinning, then was gone, lost in the flow of traffic on the highway. In a moment I followed, slowly. I had more time.

Wahoo and Goodbye

The big, white offshore boat called *Souvenir* cleared the last of the harbor boat traffic and turned south into a sweet wind coming from the open sea. Swells cleaved by the bow hissed alongside, and everywhere there were birds scribing great hunting circles in the sky or beating away on strong wings, speeding down the wind. Many of them were screaming.

"Must be hundreds," Tony Constanza said. "How many different kinds, you think?"

His friend, Frank Mariano, stood next to him at the rail.

"I don't know. Those are petrels, I think," Mariano pointed.

"What's it been, twenty minutes out, and I'm loosening up already," said Constanza. He spread a wide, strong hand over his chest and upper stomach. He was a short, powerfully built man with jet-black hair.

"You're about due to loosen," said Mariano. He was thinner, a head taller than his friend, with a jutting angular nose that gave him an appearance somewhere between a hawk and a puffin. "You bring your pills?" He pointed at the center of his own chest with a long index finger.

"Sure. Forget about it. I won't need no extra stuff out here?"

"Don't mind me asking, is it always that bad with her?" Mariano raised his chin in the direction of the shore.

"Yeah. But you ain't seen it *really* bad."

Mariano was mentally rerunning the scene of a few hours earlier, the beautiful green-eyed wife of his friend pacing like some wild cat in tight jeans, verbal razor blades slashing both of them, pausing once in awhile to scoop back her long, loose, red hair in one hand.

Constanza sighed. "Frankie, I can't afford to get rid of her, and I got just enough money so she don't leave me."

"So she's slowly killing you and cutting up the pieces with a dull knife, Tony."

Constanza glanced down the rail. There were a few other fishermen out of earshot. Mariano was the only one besides the doctor who knew about his heart. Jessica would be the last. "Jessie maybe helped with the ticker," he admitted. "I busted myself up on my own."

"For kicks?"

Constanza shrugged, remembering. The first leg, the left one, had been the worst. He knew it was broken when his friends put him back on the trail bike, telling him it was a bad sprain. He made the ride back over country that could have been used for an enduro course, the shattered knee and bones above and below it grinding against one another, finally cutting tendons, ligaments, so when they took him off the motorcycle, the whole lower leg hung loose, attached by skin and what was left of the muscles. A year and a half later when he

went over the bluff, he left the motorcycle where it was and rode back with one of his pals, his right leg braced and jutting forward. This time it was a spiral fracture that began above the knee and went close to the hip. The ankle too was broken.

That was all he wanted of trail bikes. After getting out of casts, he switched to a new road machine. It was the one on which they were trying to slap an import ban after enough kids had ridden them to oblivion on scenic mountain high-ways, in the desert, and on freeways after dark; it was the bike that catapulted from 0 to 60 miles an hour in an incredi-ble 2.6 seconds.

Constanza's printing business ran well enough and made enough to pay for the toys, the time he spent away playing with them or healing from them, and each time Frank Mariano had come to sell him film, Constanza tried to coax him on the machine for his great rushing rides out of town, into the country, anywhere. Mariano always refused. Mariano fished.

Tony Constanza once fished, too. He had never forgot-ten, and since the trouble with his heart, the days on the water in years past were more and more on his mind. He was not about to let anyone — especially Jessica — interfere with his tentative try at getting back to the old sport.

Against the rail, Constanza sucked in deep lungsfull of air, changed his stance again to ease the leg discomfort. "Yeah, Frankie," he said, "Jessie's a hundred-proof, five-letter special, all right."

T hey were seven days out now on the fourteen-day trip and had traveled well south. The fishing was slow at first, but the last day had been wonderful. They had taken a variety of fish, and the anglers stowed those they wanted below decks in the refrigerated hold of the boat. Of the species they had so far taken, Constanza liked the yellowtails best. He liked their fast streamlined attacks and the flashy good looks of them, their bright metallic blue-green backs above the brassy stripe that ran from tail through eye, and the vivid yellow tail itself that gave the sleek amberjack its name.

It was not only fish that pleased Constanza. He was becoming addicted to the intense sun that had quickly tanned him and Mariano. He was happy about the mixed group of anglers aboard, all of them getting along well, no frictions building, no inflated egos to pamper; a good group. He reveled in the salt spray that crusted and baked on them, and he was happy with the food, eating more than he should. He, Mariano and some of the others had taken to sleeping out on deck. Nowhere had he seen so many stars. He watched them stretching to the horizons while lying on his back in the sweet air that came from shore somewhere off in darkness as they held at anchor.

They were at anchor now, chumming in the bright sunlit day, hoping for yellowfin tuna but happy to enjoy whatever came along. In a ragged T-shirt as bleached as his light hair and eyebrows, captain Bud Decker watched from the bridge as the two young mates kept the chum line going. Anglers lined the starboard rail. Constanza, Mariano and a couple of others had good positions in the stern.

The two young mates moved like otters, tending the chum line, fixing containers of bait for the anglers. They were both browned deeply by the sun. Chris Flannery was quite lean but well muscled; the other mate, Mark Jarrett, was built with the smooth roundness of a long-distance cold-water swimmer. He checked Constanza's rig, made quiet suggestions, then moved to the next angler. Constanza let his bait drift back with the chum towards Mariano's line that was already well aft. The sun was hot and the ocean glassy, rising slightly now and again in gentle swells. There was little talking to break the quiet. Then Constanza heard the angler to his left utter a sudden guttural sound, saw him strike fast and hard with his short, stiff rod. Line instantly began melting from the man's reel.

"Way to go!" Constanza yelled at the angler. "What you got?"

"Big, tough one," the man said. "Gotta be one of those tunas."

Constanza was beginning to retrieve his drifted bait, reeling it in when the unseen fish hit. His rod pivoted in his grip; the butt flew up and slammed him in the stomach. He held on, leaning back, line ripping off against the drag, stunned by the sudden violence. To the right he saw Mariano's rod bending. Three of them were hooked up now, three anglers doing quick little balancing steps, following their fish, reeling and pumping when they could. The first man to hook up was forced around to starboard with his fish. Constanza and Mariano still hung in the stern.

"How you doin', Tony?" Mariano called. The fish were much heavier and stronger than those they had caught earlier in the trip.

"OK. No joke time, though," Constanza said dryly. He was up against the rail for a few moments, then was able to back away, still working on his fish. There was a sudden burst of excitement to his left, and Constanza turned briefly, saw the thin mate, Chris Flannery, leaning over with the long gaff. Then his fish began going down near the boat and he stumbled forward again.

The other angler's fish came over in one smooth swing, the gaffs of two mates in it. Constanza heard the thud as it hit wetly. Turning quickly, he saw the spotted belly, the sharp yellow flash of fins. Blood spattered brightly over the deck, hitting his leg; the fish's mouth opened as it lay dying.

Constanza was breathing hard, his mouth dry. The smooth young mate, Mark Jarrett, moved up to him.

"You all right?" the younger man asked.

"Gettin' a little winded," Constanza said.

"I do, too," Jarrett told him.

Constanza nodded, appreciating it, but feeling suddenly a little too tired. Then the fish started rising and he quickly took advantage of it, cranking fast, pumping, getting line. The fish stalled twenty feet below. He could look down and see the light shape of it, distorted by the water, the yellowfin swimming in circles.

He heard them gaffing Mariano's fish, heard it hit the deck, and then he put everything he could into his rod, and the miniature yellowfin below in the blue water began to grow larger, circling still, as he brought it up. When it finally cleaved the surface at the stern, Jarrett was on it.

Constanza stumbled back, breathing hard, his color not good, sweat running into his eyes, burning them. The fish lay before him, bright, more brilliantly marked than any other tuna, and he saw the scimitar-shaped dorsal, the vertical streaking on its flanks.

"Beauty fish," Mariano said.

"How big?" Constanza asked. His voice sounded like a raven's croak.

"He'll go eighty-five, maybe ninety," Jarrett told him. "Fine fish."

"Tony, how you feel?" Mariano asked. The mate glanced quickly at Constanza.

"I'm OK." He was breathing easier now, his color coming back. "Glad it didn't take much longer. Hey, those other fish are a lot easier."

"You got that right," Flannery, the other mate, said, coming over to help Jarrett with Constanza's and Mariano's fish. Two other anglers on the side were hooked up now, and the captain came down to help.

"Bite's on good, men," Decker said. "Get your baits back in; you don't know how long it'll last with these things."

Mariano began sending out a baited hook again.

"I'm sittin' out the next one," Constanza said. "Fight him hard for me, Frankie."

It was a good bite, and they took more tuna, but then the action slowed and died although the fish still stayed in the chum.

Some of the anglers finally switched to jigs. They tried casting them or let them drop vertically, exploring for whatever other fish might be attracted to the chum. The captain was about to call a move before heading for the evening's anchorage when the lures of two fishermen who had been casting and retrieving fast were suddenly hit.

This time it was obviously not tuna. The yellowfins had taken the bait fast, hard and down, but not with the speed at which the lines of the two anglers were now ripping from their reels. The new fish ran out rather than down, made lightening like course changes, then one of them launched itself for the sky.

"Wahoo!" someone yelled.

As though in response, the other fish exploded from the water, hurtled through the air in a tremendous leap.

The two mates moved to the hooked-up anglers, asking others to bring in their baits from the non-eating tuna.

"You see the speed of them things?" Constanza said.

The captain had come down, was behind them now. "They're a helluva fish," Decker said softly. "Jump like crazy even when they're not hooked. I've had them clear the rail on one side, sail across the stern and hit the rail on the other side dropping back in. That's just under thirty feet."

Decker checked that the gaffs were at hand, then took a long fiberglass billy from its sheath. He began speaking again, talking louder for the other anglers.

"Like to have you men leave any boated wahoo to us," he said. "If you're used to handling them, fine. But I don't want any lost fingers, or have to sew anybody up so he won't bleed to death before a Medevac can get here."

One of the fish was coming in now, and the mate Jarrett was with the angler. "When you get him to the side, just back up enough to let me in front of you," Jarrett said. "Just watch out for a last jump. Be ready if you have to duck. I've had them come right up and crash through the cabin window."

The fight of the second fish weakened suddenly, and now both wahoo were coming in simultaneously. Jarrett and Flannery moved ahead of the fishermen, reaching the long-handled gaffs, sinking the hooks, coming up and over, the two fish coming in together, hitting the deck within a second of one another.

They looked like living missiles — long, stiff, silver with blue-green backs. The wahoo beat stiffly with their entire bodies. Their mouths snapped open and shut, faceted, razor-sharp teeth cleaving, scissorlike, in counterpoint to the tattoo beaten by their long, powerful bodies on the deck.

Anglers moved quickly from the violent fish as Decker stepped in, hammering the first wahoo's head with the long, thin billy. The other wahoo skidded toward the captain's exposed ankles, its jaws working. Flannery moved in with another club, beating until the fish shuddered and was still. The two men stood up. Decker watched the fish he had subdued, reached for a folding sheath knife, then carefully pried apart the wahoo's jaws while holding the fish over the gill covers, still not trusting it.

"They don't have a shark's teeth," Decker said. "But look at how they cut against one another. Sharp as razors. Slice you up even if the fish is dead, if you're not careful. Well, we're about done, boys," he said. "We'll be heading for anchor for the night. You can fish the bottom where we're going, if you like." He climbed to the bridge. The mates tended to the anchor, cared for the fish, then began cleaning up from the day's fishing.

Constanza and Mariano sat on the upper deck looking west at the low, smoldering colors where the sun had melted below the horizon, waiting for the dark blue creeping in from the east to deepen, and for the stars to come. The two men smoked cigars Constanza had brought, drawing on them slowly.

"What a meal," Constanza said. "You don't expect pasta and sausage like that out here."

"Start coming out on these trips a little more and you'll be surprised what you get," Mariano told him.

"Why don't I do it, Frankie?"

Mariano pulled on his cigar.

"Yeah, right, you don't have an answer," said Constanza. "Damn, it was a good day. Those yellowfins are like tanks. And did you see the speed of them wahoo? You think we'll get into more of them?"

"Probably. We usually do. If you're throwing artificials, though, watch it when you pick up out of the water to cast again. Just stop for a second or two. Sometimes those things are tearing at your lure and keep right on after it if you pick up too fast. Jump right in the boat."

Constanza laughed. "Well you get them in fast, no strain that way."

"Yeah. It's no joke though, one of them things going crazy on the deck. You saw how even those beat ones are still mean as hell."

"Thanks for the tip," Constanza said.

They were quiet then. It was growing dark quickly, stars winking in, glittering in the indigo sky. The red-orange glow in the west was nearly gone. From the stern, two anglers fished sinkers and bait near the bottom.

"Hey Tony, I got a little surprise," Mariano said. "I been savin' it for after a meal I knew you'd like." He reached over into his coiled sleeping bag on the deck, and brought it out, holding the bottle up for Constanza.

"Whatta you doin'?" said Constanza. He flicked his lighter to read the label. "Grappa. Hey, is this real?"

Constanza opened the bottle and drank happily, the dry, clear, rough brandy pleasantly burning his throat, warming as it went down.

"What a way to settle the spaghetti," Constanza said. "Man, that's good. And I feel good."

"Saluté, Tony."

They sat in the dark, the ends of their cigars glowing red, and toasted the day, the fish, and the general course of things several more times.

"This is the way it's supposed to be," Constanza said. "You got me, Frankie. This is what I should have been doing instead of busting myself up for so long. I'm coming back. Now give me back that bottle. My belly feels like a drum."

He tossed his cigar into the water, hearing it hiss briefly. He did not see Mariano's grin in the dark as he handed him the grappa. Fifteen minutes later they unrolled their sleeping bags and were lying on them, the bags open and tops thrown back in the warm night. A few minutes more and they were both snoring.

The new day came in an ever-changing kaleidoscope of colors, so intense it was impossible not to stand and stare at them. And when the sun heaved up, molten orange, it lay a fiery carpet along the shimmering ocean directly toward the place the *Souvenir* was anchored. They moved to a new area not far from where the yellowfins and wahoo had been taken the day before, anchored and began chumming.

Constanza had fixed a big hammered metal spoon to his leader instead of the bait hook.

"I'm going to try for one of them wahoo, Frankie," he

said. "Those things move like something else. Not so deep to haul up, either."

"Yeah. Maybe I will, too," said Mariano. He dug a big white leadhead jig with flashy Mylar in its skirt from his tackle bag. The chum went back and the two anglers flipped their lures out, letting them sink with the chum before jerking them back. Fifteen minutes later, Mariano struck but came up empty.

"Had a bump, Tony," he said.

"Yeah? Good. Maybe they're coming in now. I'm going to see if I can get this thing out."

Constanza came back with the metal lure, being careful of his backswing, then cast hard. The compact lure lifted far aft, split the water neatly and began sinking. Constanza let it go down on a tight line, counted it down to twenty, then began a fast erratic retrieve. The shiny lure made it back untouched. He brought it in and cast again.

"Good, you do the long-distance work," Mariano said. "I'm just free-spooling, going deep with the chum and jigging back."

"I'm not going to keep this up if a fish don't bump pretty soon," Constanza told him. "This is heavy tackle to cast."

He brought the lure in and cast again, letting the spoon go down much deeper this time. He cranked hard, giving the rod long sweeps, then letting the lure flutter down. He brought the lure back almost all the way.

"Nothing," he began disgustedly. The lure was still moving, was at the stern now, and Constanza swept it up, swinging it in to cast again, and behind it, blowing the ocean apart, a huge wahoo leaped out of the water, a glittering silver projectile of nearly a hundred pounds, the sharp-pointed head, driven by the full force of the leap, lancing Constanza in the chest, slamming him to the deck, the entire fish falling on him, then skidding off onto the deck, jaws scissoring, its body beating the wood.

The captain reached the main deck in three strides, the mates moving in with him, kicking at the thrashing body of the fish, their shoes glancing off the thick slime-coat of the hard, streamlined body, keeping away from the threshing jaws, then descended on it with the clubs, beating.

Mariano leaped to his friend with an awful cry, cradled Constanza's head, trying to revive him. The huge wahoo, unworn by fighting, continued to beat violently on the deck, heaving up again, taking the blows of the billies. It took a very long time to die.

The mates and captain stumbled back from the fish. Mariano's yelled, "Gimme some help here, somebody! His heart's stopped, he ain't breathing . . ."

Decker moved in quickly, dropped to his knees and felt for the unconscious man's carotid artery. Feeling nothing, he threw himself over Constanza and commenced the pumping CPR effort to start the man's heart. Flannery ran for the cabin as Jarrett dropped to help the captain. The anglers stood in a semicircle around them.

The captain worked on the unconscious man, getting the rhythm right, Jarrett forcing timed breaths into Constanza's unresponsive lungs. Mariano talked aloud to his friend, trying to talk him back, praying him to consciousness.

Twice Chris Flannery yelled from the cabin, unable to raise a response to the emergency radio calls. In the still air, heat building, they worked a long time on Constanza, far beyond the point of hope. The captain looked at Mariano.

"He's gone, Frank," he said.

"Ah, God," Mariano cried. "Don't stop on him yet. Tony, Tony, you gotta come out of it."

Decker and Jarrett continued the futile effort, and finally it was Mariano who stopped them, acknowledging finally, putting a hand on Constanza's forehead, tears welling suddenly in his eyes.

The circle of anglers widened, no one talking as the

captain and Jarrett straightened. Mariano still bent over Constanza's quiet form. He looked up, helplessly.

"We'll have to get him below," the captain said. "It's the only cool place, in this temperature . . ."

Flannery came from the cabin wide-eyed. They lifted Constanza and carried him below to the hold where the fish were kept, resting him on the old tarp the captain brought. By the time they returned to deck, the other anglers had broken into small groups, some of the men talking softly, others just looking out to sea. Quietly, the captain gave orders, and the mates began bringing in the anchor. Mariano moved to the stern rail. He looked across the glassy ocean as far as it was possible for him to see, almost losing himself at the horizon. The others left him alone.

They traveled for forty-five minutes before the captain gave the helm to Flannery and stepped out on the bridge deck. He called the anglers together. Mariano remained aft.

"We're looking at a pretty complex situation, men," he began, "We're in foreign waters. If we can finally get through on the radio, a chopper evacuation of . . . the body is going to result in an investigation that will lock us in port for God knows how long. You know what kind of time it took us to run down here. I'm heading us back Stateside. I'll make good the remaining portion of the trip to you. If anyone wants to talk about it, please feel free to come up."

He went back to the wheel then, the anglers talking softly among themselves. Mariano looked back over the wake. Half an hour later he climbed up to the bridge.

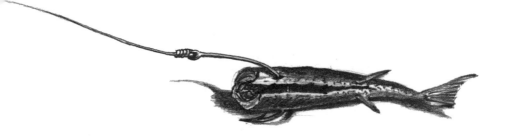

Decker turned, saw him. "Frank," he said. "What a hell of a thing."

"Yeah," Mariano said, his voice flat, sounding very tired. "Listen, Captain, I been thinking hard on this. I know Tony from a long time. I know what he would want. He would want these guys to enjoy their fishing, see . . ."

Decker was quiet a moment, then nodded. "Legally, I've got to get back," he said.

Mariano watched him, waiting.

"We might take awhile doing it, though," said the captain. "I'll speak to everyone."

And so the *Souvenir* with its somber cargo began a circuitous journey home, a trip that took in the better fishing areas that had been scheduled stops on its original itinerary. They had very good fishing in many of the places, and two outstanding days on dolphinfish and again the yellowtail. It took several days for the pall to lift. Then, slowly at first, the capsule of gloom began to crack, enthusiasm seeping back as the excitement and mechanical demands of the fishing again overtook the men. Even Mariano fished, and each fish he caught he decked in the name of Constanza.

But between fishing times a certain degree of decorum was observed. The reality of the dead man in the hold was like some dark, acknowledged family secret. It seemed to gentle the usual boisterous gusto which marked most mealtimes and evening card games. And then, on schedule, they pulled into port.

The *Souvenir* pirouetted around the breakwater, sliding to her dock, the mates tending lines smartly. The anglers stood on deck, their packed equipment collected, ready for offloading with the fish. Some waved to friends on the dock.

Standing on the bridge deck, Mariano saw her. The lovely long-legged Jessica, standing with hands on hips, perpetual irritation etching her face. Mariano wondered why she had come, had not simply waited to scream at poor Constanza when he got home. Maybe she just couldn't wait. Or maybe the cops or somebody had called her after getting the message the captain had radioed in.

They started taking off the fish, the mates and anglers all helping, and Mariano descended to the main deck and headed toward the gangway. Perversely, the old joke flashed across his mind. The story was of the fellow killed like poor Constanza in a tragic accident on a trip with friends. Unable to muster courage to inform the man's wife, the friends employed a stranger to bear the message of grief, coaching him in the gentle approach he must use. When the wife answered the door, the messenger, who did not want to waste his well-rehearsed condolences on the wrong party, queried: "Are you the widow Jones?"

Mariano giggled. He walked slowly aft. Jessica was looking fiercely at him from the dock.

"What the hell is this?" she yelled across to him. "Where the hell's Tony?"

He turned, and Mark Jarrett bumped him, running frantically with a hose, apologizing briefly, heading forward on the main deck. The captain had come down from the bridge and was moving up behind Mariano, who did not hear Jarrett's panicked voice.

"It's the dead guy," Jarrett warned the captain. "We screwed it bad back there and got the wrong side . . ."

"What are you telling me?" demanded the captain.

"Oh, God," Jarrett said, running with the hose for the hold. "We loaded all those last fish on him — he's a mess!"

Decker turned on his heel after the mate, caught the lights from the corner of his eye, the flashing lights of emergency vehicles moving silently along the pier.

Mariano started down the gangway, hearing Jessica's grating voice. Another diabolical thought had just occurred to him and he could not stop the smile on his face. What had Tony called her? The one-hundred-proof, five-letter special. Right on, Tony. He knew exactly what to do. He would present the fish, Constanza's wahoo, to her. She was just bad enough to keep it.

Home Pool

It was one of the great salmon rivers in all Maritime Canada and its first push of late summer salmon was now well upstream. Word from downriver said that another run had entered, and the water level was right, too. The only thing wrong was with Jake Chamberlain.

Maybe it was just not having fished salmon for so long, or maybe it was the way things were going for him at home, or something else. Whatever it was, his concentration was bad and his timing was terrible.

He'd had his chances the past two days and had blown them by striking too quickly or hesitating overlong. Either way it resulted in missed or lost fish. Long-time angling companion Scott Breiner, with whom he had come, was sympathetic, trying subtly to get him to relax. But Breiner had taken a limit both days, and there was that competitiveness starting to build.

Give it time, Chamberlain thought. *You've got all week and the river's wonderful and so is the camp and everything else here.*

Dinner that night in the old lodge was a rich celebration, most everyone's spirits high from a successful day astream. They were served a fine roast of beef, tender and succulent, with tall bottles of Merlot, the red wine looking smokey dark behind pale green glass and neat ivory labels. It was a festive time, made yet more pleasurable by the striking girl who served the meal. She moved with lithe efficiency, the room's mellow light accenting the lustre of her dark hair as it deepened the seasoned gold of the big log walls. Jake's eyes followed her around the room. When he spoke with her there was a responsiveness that was quick and exciting.

Dinner over, the men stood, groaning pleasurably. Scott and Jake walked out on the creaking porch. It was still quite bright. Soon the port or brandy would appear and the nightly card game would begin.

"Are you in tonight?" Scott asked.

"I don't think so. I guess I'll go watch the river some. We just had that big tide and the moon is right. More fish could have moved up by now."

"I think I'll play a few hands," Scott said. "Give me a report when you get in." They walked back inside. Jake poured himself a scotch whiskey over ice, added a little water. He went back outside and down the well-worn path to the home pool.

The far shore was in shadow, and near it in the water the humps of smooth worn boulders looked like gray bears. The pool could be extremely productive at the right times, and as he stood watching, a good fish rolled and went down. Shortly another, even larger, leaped clear, shining silver. He could feel his excitement building, the fatigue and frustration from the day, the torpor from the big meal sliding away. In a little while another fish boiled to the right on the near shore. The pool was alive with salmon. They surely would stay the night, most of them anyway. Even so, he wanted badly to fish again instead of waiting for morning. But that was not part of the routine here, whether or not you had taken your limit.

He heard the footfalls behind him, turned, and was surprised to see the girl who had served dinner. Her long hair was pulled back tightly still, but instead of the skirt she had on earlier she now wore khaki pants, a thin, pale cotton shirt covered by one of dove gray chamois cloth, unbuttoned. She had on hip boots, held a fly box and rod — a very good rod and reel, he saw at once.

"Hi," she said. "I figured there was only one way to do it, and that was to trap somebody who knows what he's doing, and you looked like the right one. Will you help me a little with my casting?"

Jake bought a moment, nodding into his drink, wondering how she had known he was there. "Sure," he said against the ice in his glass. "Casting I can do. I haven't done very well in the catching department so far."

She ignored the comment, looking directly at him.

"You might not get too much casting, though," he continued. "The pool's so full of fish you'll likely catch one."

"That would be grand," she said, "but I do need the casting practice. I never seem to keep my casts going well for too long the way you need to for salmon. What fly do you think?"

She opened the old, well-used box, and he admired the selection and quality of the ties.

"Are these yours?"

"Yes. Oh, I didn't tie them. They were my father's."

He brushed his forefinger gently across the rare feathers of the flies tied with the many materials classical patterns demanded. There were only a few in the hair-body style. Many of the older ties were on double hooks. He moved down to a fly slimmer in silhouette, far more subtle than the gaudier traditionals, so that among them it seemed perhaps plain until you held it apart as he did now, displaying its rich claret and warm brown tones.

"Try this," he suggested. "Lady Catherine."

"It's lovely," she said. "And so's the name."

"Speaking of which . . . I've been here a couple of days but you appeared at dinner tonight as suddenly as you crept up behind me just now."

She smiled easily. "I'm Devon. I was just in town a few days."

"Jake," he said.

She took the fly lightly from his fingers and bent the leader tippet to it. "I can tie it on."

He admired her quick, sure movements making the knot.

"There's a fish right over there," he pointed to a lie just up from where they stood.

"I saw it roll. Let's not try for it. Can you just help me with something first before we ruin the fish? Look, this happens a lot to me."

She shook the rod tip, working out line while pulling more from the old Hardy reel. She made several quick false casts, but then with more line extended, seemed to be having trouble.

"You see?" she said to him, turning her head and talking over her shoulder.

The sinking sun edged her profile in golden backlight and he saw she was really quite lovely.

"That's easy to fix," he told her. "That loop starts getting too big because you're coming back way too far with your rod."

He went to her, stood behind her, the water just lapping his low rubber bottom boot packs. He held the cork grip and part of the blank just above her hand.

"When you come into your backcast, stop about here, like this." The line uncurled quickly behind. "Then power forward, short stroke." Now the line snaked forward quickly in a narrow loop, unrolling straight and hard, both of them watching it, Jake suddenly acutely aware of the warm, close fragrance of her. The line checked sharply to a stop with energy enough to have gone on had there been more of it off the reel.

"It even feels better," Devon said. "You can feel it gather up a lot more power."

"Keep the line loop narrow that way," he said. "Just concentrate on that and watch the line as it goes back until you get the feel of it."

He helped her cast again several times to get the new timing down. She moved with him actively, in tune with his timing, leaning back on him as though somehow to better absorb the rhythm of his movements, and he found it totally distracting.

It took her surprisingly little time to get it right. She tilted her head against his chest and smiled back at him.

"Maybe I will catch a fish after all. Now show me that thing they do to get better distance. Heave? Is that it?"

He had let go her arm but she continued to lean on him when it suited her, as though he were a comfortable rest she was reluctant to give up.

"Heave?" he repeated. "You mean haul? Double haul?"

"I'm sure that's it," Devon said. "Would you mind?"

"We'll have to move," he said. "We'll need to get away from the branches back there, and there. Let me get my waders. The easiest thing is to just stand in the shallows."

He placed his glass on a flat rock and started back to the lodge.

"Be right back," he said.

"Be right here," Devon said.

He walked quickly up the path, blanking out hints of logic that glinted in the corners of his mind, shaking his head when he noticed the speed with which he strode up the path to the lodge. He quickly climbed the rough-sawed plank steps of his cabin, plucked his waders from their hanging pegs, and started back down to the river.

A big salmon jumped in the lie just upstream as he reached the bank. It was not a graceful, curving leap. The fish rose in a forty-five-degree angle to the surface, and when the momentum ran out, held suspended for a moment in the golden light, giving them a good look at its size and markings before it crashed back in.

"How beautiful!" Devon exclaimed.

"It was probably a hen."

"How do you know?"

"Size, and no kype. If it was a male that size, it would have a good hook jaw."

"Why do they jump that way?"

"There are a lot of ideas. Some say to get rid of sea lice, or because they're so full of energy and want to get on with spawning . . ."

"They're ready," Devon said, softly.

"You could say it," he smiled. "They come up the river stopping at different holding lies after running a rapid, or else they find a larger pool if the river is low, and wait for rain. And after they're rested from all that holding quiet, my guess is they want to get on with it."

"Show me that haul and maybe I'll try for a fish," Devon said.

"Sure." He picked up his glass, sipped, and tucked it into the inside front of his waders. "Let's move out to that shallow stretch."

They walked out little more than shin deep, the water pressing against their legs. Down the river valley a dozen kinds of birds raucously readied themselves for the night.

There was no current in the shallow backwater where they stood. Jake had Devon strip line from her reel and let it fall to float in wide coils on the surface in front of her legs. He held her rod as before and reached around her with his left hand, taking the line below the stripper guide. He had her turn slightly right and place her left hand over his line hand so she would feel exactly what he was doing in concert with the rod. He began the down and up pulls of the line to increase its speed on the back and forward cast. As soon as she was doing it well herself he had her begin to shoot the loose line between her partly open left hand after the forward power stroke. Then he held her again and showed her how to extend the aerialized line by false casting.

They waded deeper where it was necessary to hold the stripped line so it would not float in the current and become impossible to shoot. In the thigh-deep water the river pushed by them with greater force. At first he stood behind her, slightly to the left, holding the coils of line close for her, almost against her hip while she worked the haul with her left hand. Then he let her take the coils herself, learning to let them fly from her hand after the forward rod stroke. It did not take her long. He was not sure he had ever seen anyone put it together quite so quickly.

"You're really doing it well," Jake told her. "Plenty good to catch a fish. You don't need to work on any more distance than that now. That'll come. Just concentrate on placing the fly right where you want it."

"It *is* working, isn't it," Devon said. "But I sort of like it the other way."

"Other . . ."

She turned slightly and looked directly at him. "When *you* hold the line coils."

She turned back to follow her fly swinging down in the current, and at the end of its swing began stripping in line for the next cast. He picked up the slack and turned it in small and large looping coils, holding them in his left hand, and put his other arm around her gently.

"It's much nicer that way," she said.

Across the river a salmon jumped and then another followed closer to the far bank. Jake thought he saw one break the surface in the lie just upstream from where they stood.

Devon was casting casually now, lazily, really. He picked up her line with little thought, the warmth building in him.

"You could try that fish over there," he said, needing to lean only slightly forward to reach her ear.

"I'll think about it," she said. "Stay right there."

There was only the movement of the river and the sound of it engulfing them. He knew the next move would have to come, and he did not know which one of them would make it. She made another easy cast, coiled line snapping lightly from the open hand he held against her. The fly went farther out and a little farther down, and she burrowed her shoulders against his chest, happy with the cast, with everything, while they watched the line swing around and down outside the humming warmth. The next move was not theirs.

It was not an obvious lie, but had you been searching the water carefully you would probably have ventured a few casts to send a fly through the little crescent of gently bouncing water. It was big enough to hold only a very few fish. At least one was there, and it shattered the surface taking the fly solidly, their preoccupation causing just the right delay to prevent snapping the fly away from the salmon.

"Fish!" he shouted.

Devon tightened her hold on the line, coming back and up with her rod. The fish was instantly in midstream, line ripping after it in a little shower of spray as it cut the surface. The reel buzzed with the sound of a maddened cicada. And then the salmon leaped. It came up once, twice, then a third time, turned and fled downstream.

"Have you done this before?" Jake yelled.

"Not often," she answered. "I don't mind coaching."

They splashed downstream, Devon unable to move any distance out with only hip boots. She pressured the fish well and there was no need for him to give anything but encouragement. She was able to close a little on the fish before it ran out again, luckily on an upstream angle. Not far below them the current gathered, the channel compressing then funneling between a gauntlet of rocks and great humping boulders where the river finally dropped, pounding itself into a roaring white cascade.

The salmon bolted into the current, leaped again, then stalled just inside the main flow. Devon increased side pressure on the fish, gaining line, getting the fish's head around, starting the salmon moving toward her. It came in straight for a moment, then again started downstream, but in the weaker flow. She was able to turn it.

"You're doing wonderfully," Jake told her.

She smiled, but said nothing, concentrating on the fish.

The salmon made short flurries toward the main channel, but it was tiring fast, and Devon kept it from gaining confidence, parrying its efforts with smooth, steady pressure. The fish was in the shallows now. It rolled then swam in a brief circle. Jake moved for it quietly not to frighten it.

"Lift it to the top if you can," he told her. "Then ease off just a little. I'll have to hand-tail it."

She did it perfectly, bringing the salmon's head up and

over and towards her, then easing the pressure so the fish was in a horizontal position close to the surface, close to Jake. He reached down, bending over smoothly, coming over the thick, wristlike peduncle ahead of the broad tail, gripping hard, coming up smoothly and quickly with the big male, its kype dripping water, the fish looking fierce and indomitable even in defeat. He was suddenly aware of the cold wet down his front and legs, unsure for a moment, then realizing its cause, remembering the drink in his wader front. He walked toward Devon standing happily excited, and presented her with her fish.

"Thank you," she said.

She touched the salmon's flanks, acknowledging its strength and beauty. Jake took the fly, wet and dark, from its jaw. He stood there somewhat bedraggled.

"Do you want to keep it?" he asked. She paused briefly.

"Yes. I'd like this one very much."

He beached the fish, then returned to where she stood on the gravel in ankle-deep water.

"You don't need coaching," he said. "Now I'm the one who needs help." He smiled, almost apologetically, fishing the now-empty scotch glass from inside his waders and held it up.

Devon tilted her head, laughing delightedly. Upstream another salmon jumped.

"The limit is two, now, you know," she said, trying to quiet her mirth. "Actually, I know a place up river. It's not far."

Dusk was near to giving up now, and the river valley was quieter.

"That little run just below a gravel bar?"

She nodded.

"There should be fish in there, still. Probably jumping, too."

"Impatient to get on with it," Devon smiled.

They went up the path along the river, walking single file, Devon ahead. He watched her hips moving gracefully in the failing light.

It was very late when Scott Breiner returned from the card game to the cabin. Jake lay flat on his back. He listened to his friend stumble about in darkness.

"I'm awake. Go ahead put on a lamp if you like," he said. "Did you win?"

"I'll have you know that's just what I did," Scott said. "Good game."

He flopped gratefully on his bunk. "What a way to end a great day. Oh, almost forgot. There's been a change of pools for us tomorrow. We go down river instead of fishing the home pool."

"What happened?"

"Quite a few fish moved in, I guess. Well, you were down there, you must have seen them?"

"Yes. They were in all right."

"I didn't know it, but this camp is kind of a big family operation. All the staff — except for the guides — is related somehow or good family friends. So they like to let them have a full day of fishing once in awhile in the pools close by, if there aren't too many guests and it won't mean any guest fishes someplace that isn't right."

"That's nice. Sure, we'll go down river. Fine with me."

"Even the cook gets to fish," Scott said. "Oh, you know that remarkable looking lady who brought us dinner?"

"Uh-huh," Jake said carefully. He waited. Scott reached out and turned off the light.

""She's the daughter of the former owner. Coaches the rest of the staff with their fishing on the day off. Supposed to be a helluva good angler."

"I see," Jake said. He sat up, leaning on his elbows, staring into the darkened room. Slowly, invisibly, a smile worked across his face. He chuckled.

"What?" Scott asked.

"Nothing. I think I'll catch a fish tomorrow."

"You sound like it. All you needed was a couple of days to get your timing back."

"Something like that."

Bluefin Alley

T om Forrester woke in the dark, his leg cramping, head pounding from too much goombay music or maybe the final Kahlua and cream of the night. He reached down and kneaded the calf muscle of his left leg with both hands. The head and ears weren't a problem. A leg cramp was — if it hit when you were strapped to a fish that ran with the uncontrollable force of a D9 earthmover falling from a canyon wall.

In his shorts, he left his cabin and climbed the ladder to the main salon, padded on bare feet across the teak cockpit deck of his boat to look at the night. The quay of the fishing club where they were tied was dead quiet, the town street just beyond, nearly so. There was a slip of moon. Light from the courtesy lamps on the walkways illuminated undulating brown ribbons just below the surface near the transom. They appeared to be some kind of harbor flotsam until you looked more closely and saw the tiny pulsating thimble jellyfish the size of a fingernail.

A resonant snore came from below. Forrester smiled. His friend Serge Mattison was lost to the sleep goddess. He and Mattison had fished together in many places, from nameless bass ponds of the South to the crystalline steelhead rivers of the Canadian Northwest. This was their first trip together in a long time. Since the tuna.

Forrester was one of a handful of the talented for whom the tackle business had been very good. Good enough to allow him what for most men would remain just dreams. At forty-two, he had run through the world's premiere freshwater fishing; it was when he turned to the sea that he knew he'd found what he wanted. Reef fishing had given way to the demands of inshore visual stalking of bonefish and tarpon, and that led to billfish. He'd caught them all, sails to marlin, and thought that after the big blacks off Australia, there was nothing more to achieve. Then came the first bluefin. Soon he bought the forty-six foot Merritt, hired his captain and crew, earned a respected reputation and bad back in the fighting chair, and was consumed by the world of tuna hunting.

Serge Mattison had done well himself in the building trades, but his wanderings — no less adventurous — had taken him far afield of angling. Now Forrester hoped to share some of what the tuna meant to him with his friend. The timing was right for the fish. It wasn't fish keeping Forrester awake.

A few days earlier he had lost two of his crew, men who had worked for him long enough that he hadn't thought about them moving on. He hated losing them. And it worried him that of the two replacement mates his captain, Dixon Snow, had located, one was inexperienced on tuna. The other man crewed five tuna seasons aboard another boat now fishing from the island, and should be fine. He sighed, turned, and descended the ladder to his cabin.

They were all on deck now in the brightening morning, a quiet urgency upon them. Drinking juice. Tom Forrester watched them through the open doorway of the salon, watched Dixon Snow orchestrating all last-minute work. His captain was a big man. Straight, prematurely white hair worn slightly long, cool gray eyes moving constantly. The leathery-faced veteran mate Lloyd Keppler was checking baits. The captain sent the young crewman Robbie Henderson onto the quay with a Chatillon hand scale, pulling line from one of the big rods. Henderson slipped the snap swivel over the scale hook and backed up a few paces.

Dixon sat in the fighting chair. "Ready," he said. He struck against the scale twice, holding pressure the third time. Despite his husky build, the young mate obviously had to brace himself more than he expected.

"What do you get?" asked Dixon.

"Thirty-seven."

"That's high, isn't it?" Mattison was in the starboard corner watching the procedure.

"Normally," the captain said. "If we weren't using un-limited gear. It doesn't matter. With forty-three, forty-five pounds of strike drag, these fish take line as though the reel were in free spool. They just smoke it. We can slip right up to about sixty-five pounds of drag at the top." He made some adjustments and struck several more times until he had what he wanted.

"Forty-plus pounds of strike drag!" Mattison ran fingers quickly through his curly, sandy-colored hair. "What kind of leader and line are you using?"

"Usually up to number nineteen wire, about a hundred feet of three-hundred pound Japanese mono. Hundred and sixty pounds on the Dacron line. Not tournament fishing or record hunting," he grinned. "Tom likes to get them in before they overheat and kill themselves." He patted the big rod and reel. "If the angler is up to it he can keep the pressure on with this stuff and do it. Unless the hook pulls. Or the sharks get there first." He nodded at the blond mate on the quay. "That's the last one, Robbie," he said.

They had cleared the harbor, swinging south, when Tom Forrester came from the salon. They had the good wind from the southwest, just strong enough to push the sea in the direction the great fish would head. The migration of tunafish took them from the spawn up the coast to the north, to the food-rich waters where they would summer. It would angle them along the western edge of the sprawling bank in sixty feet of water, nudging them slightly toward the yet shallower water to the east. From the south to just north of the main island, a distance of 60 to 70 miles, was the slot they fished. It was called the alley.

The shallow water over the bank was the color of jade. As you moved out, the white bottom showed electric blue, then deepened to near indigo. In the neon blue of the middle depths you had the sensation of floating in space; the water was so clear you could see the bottom 80 to 90 feet below.

Tom Forrester joined Mattison in the cockpit. They stopped to watch Keppler rigging more baits — mullet with the hook through the head, beautifully sewn mackerel with the hook in the standard down position. Both were deboned. Pulled through the water, they would move like snakes. Wire leader loops held varying amounts of barrel lead at the nose of different baits. Each bait cost over $5.00 before being rigged, and the baits would keep three or four days on ice in the heat of May in this country. In a tuna-hunting operation, if your baits were not perfect, nothing else mattered.

The two men climbed to the bridge level. No one was there. The captain ran the boat from atop the tuna tower, and he had the young mate with him now.

Forrester pointed to the southwest. "We usually see them in that bright water," he said. "They look like they're surfing out there with their fins set, moving along like they're not trying. There's nothing like it. They're incredible things."

"You're tagging most of your fish now?"

"Well, releasing, anyway. They used to kill everything. We can't afford that now. But I think there are a number of boats that still might take everything they caught if they could legally sell it here like they do up north." He waved his hand to the west, toward the dropoff of the bank. "None of Reverend Moon's 'Happy World America' buy boats like you have off Massachusetts. But look at the price. A fall-caught tuna brings thousands in the States. In Japan, wholesale prices can go up to a hundred bucks a pound.

"If a fish *is* killed here, though, the word gets out instantly and the natives come to the dock with their knives and bags and they have the fish slashed down to head, tail and ribs in minutes. I mean a four- to six-hundred-pound fish!"

"That's about average size here?"

"Yes. They aren't up to top weight here like they'll get up north late in the year. We'll get some eight, nine-hundred though. Maybe it's just me, but it seems they fight harder here than anywhere. That's one of the reasons I use that heavy gear."

"Dix said something about burning out?"

"Any big fish like that can fight beyond its ability to replenish oxygen in its tissues. Tuna are strange, though, maybe more like a mammal than a cold-blooded creature. The fish thermally regulates itself — its body temperature is always a little warmer than the water. In a fight that's too long, that temperature shoots, and the fish won't recover. Commercially, it affects the flesh quality. Don't get me wrong, I'll take a fish. I just don't like to kill one when I don't have to or want to . . ."

Dixon Snow's shout from the tower shattered conversation. Mattison leaned out, looking up where the captain pointed from his perch. Forrester scanned the ocean ahead, seeing what the captain had, the sportfisherman ahead of them turning off course.

"He's baiting," Forrester said.

Forrester's boat was the second in line. The lead boat had found fish and was making its turn, positioning itself to swim its baits just ahead, but not too close to the tuna that were there. Forrester slid down the ladder to the cockpit, Mattison following, not able to make it as quickly. The captain shouted again, and the senior mate, Keppler, climbed aloft, sending the husky kid below. Mattison noticed the silver duct tape around their sunglasses, making shields along the sides of their heads and over their cheekbones to cut glare and concentrate attention, like horse blinders.

"What I'd like, is for you to handle the chair at first," Forrester said. "We don't have a big crew."

"Sure."

"Just keep me pointed at the fish; always swinging at the fish." He showed Mattison where to unlock the fighting chair. Straightening, he saw the boat behind them suddenly swing out to bait. "Look, now they're on fish!"

"What's the matter, are we blind?" said the young mate behind them. Forrester did not reply. He stayed in the chair awhile, and when nothing happened rose and walked forward. Mattison left him, climbed the ladders to the tower. Forty-five minutes later it started.

Looking up at the tower, Forrester saw Dixon Snow slap Mattison hard on the shoulder and point to port. He was in motion as Snow gunned the engines, turning hard.

There were maybe fifteen tuna, pectoral fins jutting stiffly as they slid effortlessly in the glassy water just below the surface to the port side of the boat.

Keppler was halfway down the ladder when Tom Forrester reached the chair. Mattison was just behind him. Henderson clipped the wire leader of a mackerel bait to the snap on the heavy mono line. As Mattison reached the chair the boat made a wrenching course change that nearly threw him against the starboard gunwale. He grabbed the back of the chair to stop his fall. Forrester's voice came to him calmly.

"It's a little trick," he said. "The fish don't like to cross the wake, and Dix is using it to keep them where he can see them as long as he can. You cut too close and they're gone. Did you see them?"

Mattison started to tell him. Dixon's voice cracking from the tower stopped him.

"Bait!" the captain shouted.

The young mate looped the mackerel rig sidearm and it hit the prop-churned water, going out and down. Forrester feeding line perfectly.

"Unlock the chair," Forrester ordered and Mattison bent to the lever.

"Second mark," Snow yelled from the tower.

Forrester continued feeding line until the second mark passed through the tip guide. Now he slapped his left hand over the line against the thickness of the powerful butt, feeling the bait swim, feeling for the barracuda or other quick, sharp-toothed fish that would soon come to destroy the mackerel.

"There!" Keppler shouted.

They could see the tuna from the cockpit now, sailing high in the water, aft and just inside the wake.

"Cut," Forrester snapped. He cranked the gold Fin-Nor reel hard, bringing in the cleanly severed bait.

"Cuda," he said. "You see it?"

"No," said Mattison.

Behind the boat the pod of huge tuna swam easily with the northern current and the steady breeze blowing with it. They were conscious of the whine of distant boat engines. The sounds of the engines did not trigger alarm as would the pinging of hunting killer whales. They were simply aware of them as they would be of the deeper vibrations of a large shark which posed no threat to them with their great speed and agility. They were older fish that had survived long enough for their year class to be reduced considerably. Compared to schools of smaller fish that might number in the hundreds, these larger tuna swam in pods of a few individuals. The lead fish of the group was a giant female that Dixon

Snow, in his loft high in the tower, knew must weigh at least nine-hundred pounds.

She was the first to see the mackerel bait tumbling downward through the water. The bait continued sinking as the tuna approached, then snapped from its lazy descent and shot upward and away in an erratic swimming motion. Then something very strange occurred. The frenzied mackerel did not veer away in attempt to escape. Instead it continued to swim about 250 feet ahead of the tuna.

Watching it, the pod of tuna continued on their course. Driven by the need to migrate, they had not eaten for some time. The bait that swam so strangely before them did not elicit the feeding urge that a sizeable school of forage might have, but the frantic snakelike movement of it signaled distress, signaled helplessness, and that excited the giant fish.

Either their excitement caused the tuna to move faster, or the mackerel was falling behind. It did not matter. The strange, taunting fish was closer, and finally it became irresistible. Sudden energy surged through the lead female; she left her pod in a sweeping rush and engulfed the bait.

The tuna humped up through the ocean surface, her back showing darkly slick as she took the bait, going down with it, turning, suddenly feeling shock after shock in the right corner of her mouth as Forrester set the hook. Her reaction to the jarring force was instant flight. So violently did she wrench her body away from the danger, that the tuna behind her scattered in fright.

Her flight took her over clumps of dark bottom growth and white sand that seemed to waver from sinuous ribbons of water-filtered sunlight crossing it. Now in the shadowy distance ahead, she saw the gloom and

darkening color of the water that meant the edge of the bank, the sanctuary of depth. The holding force was still with her as she rushed for the crags at the edge of the escarpment which first dropped to a hundred fathoms, and after that screamed down over two thousand feet.

On deck, the violence of Forrester's wordless striking had stilled the voices of the others. Almost as the fish began its run, Dixon Snow rammed the throttles to their forward stop, spun the wheel to send the speeding boat to the edge of the bank. Even if the fish had stayed longer in the shallower water, he knew it would ultimately make its final bid for freedom in the depths. Now he had to reach the edge before the descending line would touch the craggy wall of the drop and abrade against it. He ran the boat on a parallel course with the tuna, and the line knifed through the water in a bow he tried to keep from becoming too large.

Mattison worked to keep Forrester pointed at the fleeing fish while Keppler ran up the red fighting flag. Line ripped from Forrester's reel with speed that shocked Mattison. When they reached the edge and the deep, snag-free water, he thought they would quickly gain advantage, but then he looked again at Forrester's reel.

Line still ripped from the spool, going both out and down while Snow turned the boat's transom in the direction of the sounding fish. Mattison realized their only gain was having avoided the cutting edge of the bank.

Diving with all her power, the giant tuna left the light of the surface and with it the closing thunder of the boat engines. She passed through fifty fathoms at an incredibly steep angle of descent, aware that the frightening pull against her was increasing. The ocean light grew fainter as she continued ever downward, knowing only to flee until she could do

so no longer. In the silence and scant twilight near a hundred fathoms,
she was forced to stop.

Five hundred yards of line had been taken from Forrester's
reel, and now the fish began to lash against the unknown
thing that held it. The tuna's violent jerking sent shocks into
Forrester's body and took yet more precious yardage in short
wrenching spurts. Still the boat backed down toward the
place where the fish had sounded. Since striking, Forrester
had simply held while the fish ran. Now he threw his reel
into its low gear and commenced to fight.

He gained perhaps fifteen yards before the fish took
them back again along with a little more. He did not try to
stop it, but the moment it stalled he began his pumping
again, tenaciously, legs and arms and back working in
rhythm, putting all his weight into it.

Dixon Snow had moved from the tower to the bridge,
where he delicately positioned the boat from time to time,
continuing to handle the controls behind his back as he
watched the angle of line to the fish.

The sun had heated the day to over one hundred degrees
but the steady southwest breeze evaporated the sweat now
pouring from Forrester's body. He had pumped up over two
hundred yards of line, but the fish had not truly tired or
begun to circle. It was only allowing itself to be lifted by the
relentless pressure, not in pain, only resting from its sustained run, the strain of the dive and the great pressure of the
extreme depth. Then it began to dive again. Not frantically,
but steadily, irresistibly, not just down but slightly away. It
took all the line Forrester had regained, and when it had, the
angler did not wait any longer for the fish to stop but braced
his body against the force and was pulled from his seat, holding above the chair a moment, legs and back taking it all. He
stopped the fish.

Forrester had strained himself to a point of internal
bursting, and now could not stop. Stalling the fish was his

opening and he took it, pumping again, faster, short smooth pumps that for the first time caused the fish to turn. He kept the rhythm going as long as he could, and during his sliding lifts from the fighting chair, Keppler squeezed a bottle of liquid soap over the seat.

"Now you can scoot like a greased watermelon seed, Mr. Forrester," said Keppler.

The increasing pressure from the line that caused the giant tuna to halt forward effort, also caused her to turn toward the side where the hook was imbedded in her mouth. The movement immediately eased the relentless pull, but relief lasted only moments. The pressure came again, and she instinctively turned from it. As the pull increased beyond her ability to fight it, she yielded once more, and in doing so began the first arc of what would be the first great circle of her defeat.

Three hundred feet above and perhaps a third of a mile distant, another fish had begun circling, too. Instinctively responding to the distressed beats of the tuna, it now sought the source of those vibrations, circling again, then beginning a quartering sweep toward the hooked bluefin. As it quartered, it also began descending. The fish was a tiger shark of nearly seven hundred pounds, and though it was alone in the deep water, it was not the only shark sensing the tuna's struggle.

From the shallower water over the bank, three others had responded to the distress sounds of the bluefin. Yellow-brown, with broad snouts, they were lemon sharks, and though nowhere as big as the tiger, their vicious nature well made up for size. Now they began their approach toward the area where the tuna was fighting.

On each inward arc of the bluefin's circle, Forrester wound more line. On the going-away segment, he attempted to keep the strain great enough so the tuna would swim slightly canted, causing its pectoral fins to lose their effectiveness, especially for diving. On each circle he brought the fish a few feet higher in the water column.

When they spoke in the cockpit, their voices were low but taut. Since gaining his advantage, Forrester had not said a word nor stopped his machinelike pumping. Now as Keppler poured water over his head and down his back, he cracked his silence.

"Give me some I can drink," he said.

Robbie Henderson went for the near icebox, grabbed one of the water jugs and held it for Forrester to drink. Though the angler tilted back his head, he never eased pressure on the fish.

The giant tuna had been lifted from the twilight depths and into the zone where shafts of sunlight penetrated from the glittering surface far above. Like light through high cathedral windows, the rays of sun stretched and flickered into the blueness of the water, playing over the silvery flanks of the great tuna as she circled.

On her next outward arc her excellent vision showed her the shadow of the tiger shark at the edge of light. She knew what it meant and doubled back on her swing, lunging again in attempt to free the hook. The sudden slack was so quickly taken up that it tipped her further to the side at an angle, enabling her to see, above, the silhouettes of the three lemon sharks against the polished ocean surface. The three scribed broad arcs of their own, their circles far larger than hers.

The tunafish broke from her spiral, sacrificing depth to gain distance between herself and the waiting sharks. The effort drained her strength. It also gained her space, but now she was vulnerable to anything from below. She was stalled just beneath the surface.

At the first violent lunges Forrester knew something had frightened the fish. When the tuna ran, taking line but climbing toward the surface, he knew it must be sharks. Nothing else would cause the bluefin to sacrifice depth just to gain distance from the boat. He understood what the fish's effort cost it, and increased his own once more, pushing the drag lever forward slightly, lifting faster, feeling a quick pain in his lower back. The stalled tuna had not yet recovered. Unable to resist, it turned toward the hook, slid the rest of the way to the surface and broke through.

They saw it suddenly from the boat, crying out as one voice from the hugeness of it, saw the dark steel blueness of its back, the gleaming silver of its flanks as it rolled off balance, then fell below the surface again, starting away.

Dix gunned the engines, backing down, backing fast, Forrester cranking at speed, the reel in high ever since the fish moved up, and now the mono was spooling in, wet and shining like a strand of glass through the guides onto the reel, water dancing from it in the sun.

The boat turned, running parallel with but behind the tuna, Mattison keeping the chair pointed perfectly, and now the fish was up again, scant feet below the surface, looking huge, showing plainly in the air-clear water but distorted by the rippled surface and dappling of the sun. Forrester slammed the drag lever toward the horizon.

He cranked to keep the fish up as they closed on the giant bluefin, and when they were upon it, Mattison saw, over Forrester's shoulders, the huge complex eye of the great fish. Then it was gone, the young mate Henderson slamming in front of them, ahead of the senior Keppler, wanting the wire leader for himself.

They were using only slightly more than fifteen feet of wire for the leader, and so it was possible to take a grip, and in one smooth, powerful effort, bring a beaten fish sliding to the boat. Robbie Henderson had the wire in his cotton-gloved hands, took the bend carefully for extra purchase, and attempted to bring the great fish to them. With the gaff, Keppler moved smoothly, anticipating the striking position, began rounding the fighting chair behind Forrester and Mattison, and when he was clear again, he saw it was not right.

The fish had begun sliding to them, but either its weight or last throbbing resistance had stopped it, causing Henderson to stumble into the gunwale. He shifted his grip on the leader, the wire looping up for a second on his forearm, then slipping back as he pivoted into the cockpit, pulling.

Watching from the bridge, Dixon Snow saw the tuna's tail begin to beat, shouted the warning below as Henderson's new leader grip slipped and the wire slid beneath his left-hand glove, a perfect loop tightening around fingers and hand, a severing noose. Snow was at the ladder to the deck as the leader tightened.

The young mate's scream ripped through the air. He clawed with his free hand, trying to reach the leader above the noose, the brilliance of his blood against the blue water and tanned skin shocking him further, shocking them all. He could not reach the leader and was pulled back by the fish toward the gunwale, screaming again.

Keppler flung the gaff, moved for the stricken Henderson, but the captain pushed him aside, grabbed the three-hundred-pound test wire, pulled it down, cutters in hand, while Henderson screamed in agony. The captain looked at Forrester, asking silent permission. Then the fish moved and somehow Henderson's hand was free. The young mate dropped to the deck, all of them seeing the flash of mangled fingers, the quick white of bone, before he ripped at his own shirt to wrap and hold the ruined hand. He crabbed across the deck on his knees, whimpering, smearing the bright blood trail he was leaving on the silvered teak.

It had taken moments, but it was enough time for the tuna. The huge fish rolled, its rear dorsal slicing up, finlets and scimitar tail following as it dove. Forrester was thrown up from the chair, the clublike rod bending hard for the water before he eased the drag. Line poured from the reel.

The tuna no longer had the strength for a sustained run or dive to the depths she had earlier attained. She understood only to take advantage of the decreased pressure and small amount of new energy the brief pause had allowed to course through her body. She dove as far as she could and saw the tiger shark coming in. It swam with easy beats of its big tail, pectorals out, mouth slightly open, directly at her right flank. In the instant before it rolled up to strike her, the tuna writhed with violence that momentarily frightened the shark. It cut short its attack and swam out in a large arc.

On deck Forrester punched the drag lever forward again. The telegraphed violence of the tuna's movements were clear to him.

"I don't know how badly that leader's kinked," he said. "I hope bad enough to break now." And then he felt the thudding vibrations through the line and rod, and knew that it no longer mattered.

It had not been the tiger but one of the lemon sharks of the group of three. Coiling and circling, they had dropped to where the tuna held suspended, and the largest of the three had risen on the left from below while the tuna watched the shadowy form of the tiger shark coming back again. The lemon struck just forward of the tuna's vent, piercing the intestinal wall of the giant fish, holding on and shaking the length of its body to tear tissue, fat and entrails free. At once a cloud of blood exploded in the water, rusty brown at this depth. Seconds later the big tiger shark struck, cutting a great crescent of flesh from the tuna's forward flank behind the pectorals.

Forrester cranked furiously, cursing the sharks, wanting to deny them any more of the fish — a fish they could never have taken had it not been hooked.

"Get that transom door ready, and gaff!" he yelled. "Get anything you can grab to keep the bastards off. Go help them," he ordered Mattison.

The bluefin was coming up straight behind them, its highly wrought cardiovascular system pumping and pumping out blood that billowed through the water, driving the sharks into frenzy. By the time it reached the surface, the tuna was dead.

The sharks came with it, circling crazily in the reddened

water, Forrester cranking still. One of the lemons came again, tearing at the carcass, and then the entire sickening carnage was at the stern of the boat. Mattison had the boat hook. He stood beside Keppler with the gaff. Together they beat at the lemon sharks churning the surface to a red froth. Then the tiger moved in, rolling up, scraping the props, knocking into the transom door as it locked onto the fish. Dixon Snow reached down with the fixed killer gaff, grabbing for the big shark.

"Stinking, rotten. . ." he began, coming up with the ten-inch hook into the underside of the tiger. The Shark still held on. Snow freed the gaff hook and struck again to break its hold. The big shark went down.

Keppler had the transom door open now, and they were reaching with gaffs, Mattison still slamming at the water with the boat hook. They managed to get the head and shoulders of the bluefin through the door, then Keppler had to rope it and fix the rope to the winch Dixon secured to the boat. The rest of what was left of the tuna came in. Mattison stumbled to one side, then saw the dorsals of the lemon sharks cutting the surface three feet from the transom. He reached out with the hook, slashing at them in rage until he realized the pressure on his shoulders was Forrester's grip. He nodded, turning, started for the cabin, saw the young mate lying inside the door, eyes closed, the ruined hand wrapped in towels. It was a long trip back in.

On the scales of the fishing club the remains of the tuna weighed six hundred and sixty pounds. Whole, the fish would have gone over nine hundred.

"I don't know if the locals will touch it after the sharks," Forrester said quietly. "But we'll leave it."

When they passed by later, what was left of the fish was so black with flies that Forrester could not bring himself to look long enough to tell if they had taken the good meat with their knives and plastic bags. Both men were silent as they headed for the bar.

Jimmy

We motored quickly through the chop in big freighter canoes, the twin-engine Canso that had brought us in spinning on its floats behind us, turning into the wind that came in from the sea, into the broad estuary. The boats crunched up on the gravel beach and the guides immediately began the offloading and then onloading of the guests of the previous week who were going out as we came in. I stopped one fellow to ask about the fishing.

"We had both good and bad," the man said. We exchanged some pleasantries before we got into some valuable details on the better spots. He wanted to know where I was from, and when he learned that I lived near him, produced one of his business cards. It said Pierre Joilette, Hypnotist.

"Yes, it's true," he said. "Besides the usual performances — for entertainment, you know — I do a bit of post-
hypnotic therapy. Entirely without license. Look me up if
you're in town."

He climbed into the freighter canoe and waved. I started
walking up the rough plank walkway toward the camp buildings along with other guests, while guides moved past for
more of the duffel. Ahead of me, halfway up the incline, two
fishermen I had not yet met were looking back at the estuary
where the plane was taking off. They were carrying a lot of
small personal gear — bags, binoculars and the like. One, a
short, stocky, swarthy fellow in a mackinaw, had a cassette
player hanging around his neck. They had placed some of
their gear on the walkway and the short fellow was taking
slow, deep breaths. As they watched, the plane left the water.

I was pretty well laden with gear myself and started
around the two men, wanting to drop the things, get orga-
nized. I greeted them.

The short fellow jabbed a finger at his chest. "Bum
ticker," he said, the voice gravelly and dry. "Tell them to save
a bunk for us."

"You ought to let the guides carry all this stuff for you," I
said. "They'll do it. Here, let me give you a hand . . ."

"Nah, nah, you're loaded down already," said the one in
the blanket coat, and I grabbed his small travel bag, slinging it
over a shoulder.

"We'll be right along," the taller of the two said in a voice
like new velvet. I went on ahead.

There was the usual hangup while the camp manager
assigned sleeping quarters for the week. He called off two
more names just as the fellow in the mackinaw and his pal
were reaching the top of the walkway. The short fellow with
the heart problem rasped at the manager.

"That's us," he said. "Where do we bunk?"

The steepness of the incline had obviously been an
effort for him. The manager welcomed them, pointed to the

nearest of the rough cabins. I gave him back his bag.

"Thanks," he said. I couldn't believe the voice. "Hey, where are you sleepin'?"

It wasn't a full camp and the manager was breaking up the group, giving parties the luxury of separate quarters. He had assigned me to the wall tent up on a little knoll, and I pointed to it.

"Ain't there more room in our cabin?" he asked the manager.

"Oh, yes," the man said. "I thought maybe you and Dr. Edwards might like the extra space and privacy."

"Ah, we know each other too good. Put him in there, too — unless you *want* the tent," he said to me.

I didn't care. I just wanted to fish. "No, that's great. Thanks. I won't have to come on down to your cabin for a shower."

"Thanks for lugging the bag," he said.

The doctor went in, his friend motioning me ahead. I grabbed the wood-frame screen door while his friend started grousing behind me.

"Geez, how do you survive?" he asked.

"What?"

"Never mind; go ahead in."

I was stepping inside when he jostled me from behind, grabbing the door to hold it open. He apologized for the bumping. The doctor had already placed his things on one of the benches at the long table and was rolling out his sleeping bag on a lower bunk.

"Here's what I mean about surviving," said my new friend. He offered the brown leather wallet-looking folder that I had been carrying in a rear pocket.

"You carry this stickin' out like that, you're easier than a park pigeon to knock off. What, don't you *like* money?"

He'd surprised me all right.

"Sure," I said, "but I wouldn't carry it like that. This is a notebook."

"Maybe you ain't so dumb, then," he grinned. "Hey, no offense. You grow up in the streets, you always see things like that. I just don't like to see anybody get took so easy. What's your name?"

I told him. He said to call him Jimmy. He told me the last name, but it's not important. The doctor was Carl Edwards. Everybody called him Doctor Ed. They had come to fish, of course, but it was soon evident that the need to put some space and time between themselves and the way things were back home was equally important.

The two men, seemingly so different at first, were high-school classmates from Brooklyn. Not from what you would call one of the better sections. Out of their graduating class of young men and women, seven made it past the age of thirty. I wanted to ask why neither of them had left, but you didn't ask that kind of thing.

"Still there," I said.

"Still there," said the doctor.

"Who can leave?" Jimmy said, then began filling Doc Ed in on the most recent loss among the surviving seven. When he was finished he turned to me. "We're like an endangered species or something," he said. "So we kind of keep track of whose left and tick them off as they go."

It was arctic char country, but there were some fine brook trout, too, in the headwaters and smaller tributaries. From the base camp it was a good hike to one section on the main river that the hypnotist suggested we try. Or you could take a freighter canoe down most of the way, then walk. That's what Jimmy, Doctor Ed, and I did.

Jimmy wanted a char. He fished hard, shooting his favorite little spinner out to swing round in the slow currents, and at an especially good pool Doc Ed and I sat on a boulder, talking as we watched him.

"I hope he takes a beauty sometime this trip," Doc said. "I don't know how many more he has left."

"It's that bad?"

"He's had two big ones, plus a couple near episodes. The heart is an awfully tough piece of equipment, but there's not much of his left."

"He always have troubles?"

"No. No, that's the thing of it. Hell, he handled everything all his life. The neighborhood was — is — something not everybody handles. Let me tell you, this is the kind of place where when I have emergencies at the hospital late nights, I don't stop at traffic lights. They come at you in the middle of an intersection, and it doesn't matter that you have the door locked. I have the revolver now, but still I don't stop. That doesn't impress him; never did. It was the horses. Well, maybe he'll tell you about it sometime."

Doc Ed got up and stretched, then headed down to the water to his friend.

In the evenings in the small cabin, I learned something of the basic skills a kid acquires growing up in Jimmy's and Doc's neighborhood. Besides lifting a wallet, stashing a billy or knife so it could miraculously appear in hand with one oil–slick movement, there was the business of working over a card deck in several ways, though Jimmy was as honest as fresh-fallen snow during our nightly games. Surprisingly, along with the city street stuff, he'd also started hunting and fishing early. As a kid he supplied his house and some close neighbors with fish from Jamaica Bay and Long Island Sound, and ducks from the rich wetlands where Kennedy airport now sprawls.

After awhile I gained some insight into the subtleties of serious money-laundering systems. By and by when talk got around to rigged sporting events, I asked Jimmy if he followed and played the games.

"Not any more," he said.

We were getting to know one another pretty well on an easy level, but not all doors opened. Jimmy finished his hand and leaned back, reaching for that little Sony Walkman he always kept close like some kind of touchstone. He had one favorite tape by Earl Garner, and one favorite piece on the tape. It was the song Misty. Often, he hummed fragments of it, along with the tape. Sometimes he'd hum as he walked to a fishing spot with the machine turned off.

"I guess that's it for me, tonight," he said abruptly, and took the tape player outside. Doc slid the cards together. Jimmy was up on us about three bucks. After awhile I went out too, for a last look around before going to bed. It was cool outside; the normal cloud cover had blown away and there were so many stars glittering against a perfect velvet black sky that you just had to stand and stare awhile and shake your head at the richness of it. Jimmy came around the corner of the cabin then and saw me.

"Hey," he said, "I didn't mean to cut you off in there. You just hit the big screwup in my life. I should give you an answer. Yeah, I put bucks on the games. Just one, though, just on the horses. That was plenty. That was everything . . ."

We eased down the wood walk that ran past all the cabins, the cook and dining buildings, supply and generator sheds, and I heard about the horses.

Jimmy had been a regular, a disciplined regular, but for too long. He had fallen into the small-time bettor's trap. He'd learned racing as well as you can, and was winning often enough over the long haul, but a two-dollar bettor who stays with the favorites can win a handful of races and show a profit of maybe $30 if he's lucky. The rush was gone. The palms no longer sweated. So he upped the ante — and began hunting for long shots. He won some good ones, but long term, the attrition began. Losses piled on losses.

The debt became a thing beyond his handling. Inevitably there came the last-ditch chance that would bail him out. It was classic long-odds stuff, arranged and guaranteed. Sure it was a fix, but his troubles were well known, and he was inside. He was also totally desperate.

The horse was Golden Shamrock with a record of scattered, glittering performances in an overall undistinguished career. Like the majority of horses, he was running on bute. Phenybutazone the anti-inflammatory drug used in place of rest to disguise, to numb an animal's pain in muscle and joint, to keep the walking wounded going for one more race. Bute had replaced aminopyrine when it was found that the later had the potential to destroy bone marrow. And in just this race, Golden Shamrock was possibly running on something extra.

The gelding made his move just as the sun slipped from behind a cloud edge, washing the track and the horses in coppery, dusty elegance. The horse pulled from a knot of four that had been running as one, and steadily began closing on the favorite, who was tight on the rail and not all that far out front. The crowd was on its feet now, roaring in a single voice, none louder than Jimmy's. The Shamrock went past the stand, neck stretched, nose passing the right boot of the jockey just ahead, and there was the sound of a gun firing that was not the detonation of primer and powder, but the exploding of Golden Shamrock's left front leg.

The horse went wildly out of control, unable to stop, his momentum carrying him forward while the lower part of the ruined shin and the hoof, both still attached to the horse by skin, dragged on the track. The jockey frantically, futilely tried to rein him, then kicked both boots from the stirrups and dove off. You could hear him hit the track solidly. He rolled for the rail just before the knot of three horses with which Shamrock had been running thundered past, those further back turning out, away from the horror.

Shamrock slowed, pitched forward about to go over, but caught himself. He stopped, then tried to move ahead, lurching on three legs and the stub of bone. The horse stopped again, facing the stands in confusion, his breath coming hard and fast. A trainer ran for him, got the reins, tried to comfort him, rubbing his head, holding him there. The meat wagon came in minutes.

The two men rolled fast from the van, running for the back, opening the rear doors of the van, lowering the ramp. They ran to the horse and trainer, tried to start Golden Shamrock moving. Blood ran down around the exposed bone, dripping where the fetlock had been, and with prodding the horse attempted a few steps but its pain was too great. It turned its head in fear now, the trainer still at the reins, and refused to move. The men from the van went behind, held a double rope sling across the horse's rump, pulling hard enough to get the animal moving. It lurched up the ramp and the ragged bone dragged, grating on the metal. They closed the doors on Golden Shamrock's life and drove away.

Jimmy stood holding his racing notes, feeling a weakness suddenly in legs and stomach, then the cold all the way through him, knowing it was over, knowing the one thing left for him to do.

We reached the end of the walkway in the star-filled night and Jimmy stopped talking for a minute. He had been facing straight ahead all the while he spoke. Now he turned to me suddenly, his voice sounding worse than usual.

"So, I got into trouble, and there ain't no more games, see, 'specially no horses. Just the fishing. I still talk about the fishing. How about we go back now." He briefly placed a hand on my shoulder.

The next day we headed for the outpost camp. That was the way they ran things. If you started at the waters of the main camp, at mid-week you went back into the interior, rotating with other anglers who had already been at the outpost camp. It was a long ride by boat. The weather was gray and I pulled on my dark-blue rainjacket and yanked up the hood. I was alone with one guide; Jimmy, the Doc and their guide were in the other freighter canoe. After half an hour running, I could see that the country was not going to change any and I took out a book to read. The foul-weather gear blocked the wind, and I was happy that it wasn't raining yet.

Suddenly we veered to the right, and I slammed back to reality. There was a loon dead ahead, something obviously wrong with it. Instead of diving or flying off as we bore down on it, the bird flapped and kicked along the surface. I yelled at the Inuit guide, waving one arm, trying to call him off, but we slammed ahead over the bird, which made one final effort to sound, but I was sure we hit it. It was a matter of how hard. We turned sharply back on course then, and I wheeled around to see the guide grinning. I wasn't smiling.

I yelled, trying to get an answer, some reason for a mindless act. He looked puzzled. Through a combination of hand motions and a few words, he finally understood that I wanted to know why, and he gave me his answer, a shrug of the shoulders. Something to do. A fat, fed cat cuffing a songbird to death, latent instinct rising. I didn't much like where this was going and went back to my book. Maybe another half hour had passed before I heard Jimmy yelling at me off the port side. Their boat had been behind most of the trip but was now alongside and Jimmy was saying something I couldn't get until he had his guide move closer.

"Hey, you look like a priest in that getup. That your bible?" He jabbed his arm indicating the book in my lap.

I couldn't help laughing.

"Sure," I said. "I'll pray for a trophy for you."

We hit a wave and spray sloshed over both of us.

"That hood's not so dumb," Jimmy yelled. "Father Flanagan," he invented, pulling up the collar of his blanket mackinaw. "I should have dug out rain gear, too."

Their boat pulled ahead and I watched them for awhile. After that I was Father Flanagan.

We put our gear in order in the small cain of the spike camp. Jimmy was tired after the trip and wanted a nap instead of fishing. He said he might join us a little later. The guide who ran my boat went out to cut firewood; the other one took a net and went with us to the river that here was more like a lake.

"What's your guide's name?" I asked Ed.

"Jason."

"Jason," I said, turning to him. "You fish char there, up and down from the narrows?"

The man nodded. "Char here," he said, pointing generally at the narrow section above an island, and also below the island where a big pool fanned out. "Big char in pool," he said.

We took a couple of char each, nothing big, but the guide wanted them for supper. We'd eaten a lot of fish this trip, but with char the featured course it would be a long time before I became bored with it. The gray light was fading quickly, and Jason walked to the little depression he had made in the shallows for the char, hooked fingers through the gills of the fish we had kept. We waded in, grabbed our gear bags and followed him up the path to the little cabin. Stepping inside, the warmth, good cooking smells, Jimmy's broad smile and vast enthusiasm, swept us up. He was well rested, excited to fish, and wanted to know all about the new water. He listened carefully when we described it to him, nodding his head.

"It's good," he said. "I feel good about it. Maybe this is the place. Yeah, I think maybe this is the place where I'll get him."

Later that evening, warm from the food, a drink and the fire that crackled in the little sheet-metal stove, Jimmy waited until Ed had gone out, then told about another dream.

"Doc and me been on some good trips," he said. He sat near the stove, hands folded across his belly, feet up on one of the benches of the eating table. "I doubt I'm up for many more big ones like this, but I'll tell you what. Doc's building a vacation home in New Hampshire. He showed me the plans. There's an extra room, with a balcony, yet. He didn't need no extra room. He's makin' it just for me for when I come to visit and fish. There's pretty good trout fishing near there. But ain't that somethin'? He thought enough to make a special room for me. He's some kind of guy, Father Flanagan. Don't matter he's a famous doctor — he don't forget an old friend. I'm already making plans for when I get up there."

Jimmy liked the look of the island pool right away. Ed and I watched him wade out, looking solid and sure. He waved and called back once he was ashore.

"I'm gonna just plant myself here for the morning," he announced.

Ed went back to the place he fished the evening before, and I took a hike, looking for some good trout fishing. I found it, too, one of those times and places you never forget.

Ed was on the bank opposite the island when I reached the big river. On the island stood Jimmy and the guide Jason, his big empty net wet and obviously just emptied of the prize Jimmy now clutched like a whole salami of gargantuan proportions against his blanket mackinaw. It was a beautiful char, predominantly silver, the first blushes of spawning red touching its flanks. Jimmy was grinning like a little kid, but it was plain that Doc Ed was just as happy.

"Hey Father Flanagan, how about this?" Jimmy yelled across to me. "This is the baby I've been waiting for; this is the one I'm taking home."

"Great fish!" I shouted over the river. "Are you coming across or going to fish more there?"

"Just gonna rest a little before I cross."

The guide offered to take the char over to the main bank, but Jimmy was having none of it. He was keeping the fish right there with him. He sat down with it.

"I've got a scale," I yelled. "I'll come over there and weigh it if you'd like."

"Yeah, do that and congratulate me, too."

I took the Chatillon scale from my kit bag, and Ed and I waded quickly across.

Jimmy sat looking happy but tired, one arm draped over the fish. We shook hands all around, including Jason whom Jimmy wanted close by with the net to take the char back across when he was ready. For now he wanted to sit and rest and think about it some more. The man was so happy it was contagious.

"What did he take?" I asked.

"This," he held up the little spinner. "My favorite lure."

I shook my head looking at the little hooks.

"You must have played it gently."

"He was on it almost half an hour," said Doc. "And wore himself out doing it."

"Worth it," Jimmy beamed.

"If you'll let go a minute I'll weigh it," I offered.

"If you're quick."

I slipped the scale's hook under one gill, hefted the big male, read the non-metric side of the brass tube. "You did all right. Fourteen pounds even."

"Good," Jimmy said. "Give it back. What's the record?"

"I'm not certain, offhand."

"This is the record," he said. "This is the biggest fish of my life."

The big carefully wrapped char made it back home,

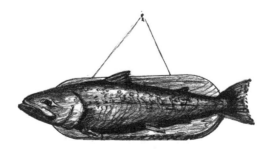

along with the rest of us and all the equipment. I sent Jimmy a couple of photographs I had taken of him, Doc and the fish. I didn't hear from him, and didn't expect to, though he had promised we'd have dinner one day at a special place — "the best Italian food you'll eat," he said. But a lot of promises are made at camps. I was surprised when the phone call came. There were no preliminaries, no introductions.

"Can you get yourself over here on Thursday, Father Flanagan?"

I hadn't heard the gravelly vice for two months but I knew who owned it.

"How's the char mount coming," I asked.

"It's done! It was supposed to be finished in maybe eight to twelve months, but I put some muscle on the taxidermy guy. It's somethin' beautiful, all right. I got it at my house. You coming to dinner Thursday or not?"

"Sure. Where do you want to meet?"

"My place."

At first I thought he meant his home, but he gave me the address in Manhattan, then told me when to meet him. When I found it, I could not fault Doc Ed's description. Through sheer luck, there was a place to park close by. I locked the car and headed to the building. There were six steps up from the sidewalk. The front door opened almost smack against the receptionist cubicle. A heavyset older woman looked at me through dirty glass with one of those talk holes in it.

"Are you the guy Jimmy's waiting for?" she asked. Her voice had the musical lilt of a greasy wrench.

"Hope so."

She pressed a hidden buzzer and I could hear it sounding off somewhere behind partitions not far away. Jimmy came right out.

I don't know what I was expecting; maybe the blanket mackinaw or the dark wool watchcap he had worn up north. It was Jimmy, but not Jimmy. Not the one I thought I knew.

"Father Flanagan," he said, sticking out a hand. The

voice was still the same. He wore a gray sport jacket with a complex checked pattern, gray trousers, no tie, and his color did not look good. Then he smiled and the grin lit his face, and that looked right, but a little seriousness remained.

"Hey, long time. It's good to see you," he said. "I got somethin' for your wife or girlfriend or whoever." He went in behind the glass where the woman sat and came out with a bolt of good-looking plaid fabric. "Maybe she can make a dress or something out of it. It's top stuff."

I thanked him.

"Let's get out of here. We're going to get into traffic but I know a couple short cuts. My car's outside, you can follow." He turned to the silver-voiced receptionist, who was watching us impatiently behind her glass barricade. "Go ahead, close up, Angel," he told her. "Okay, let's go."

He pointed out his car, a big old cream-colored Mercury across the street. We started down the steps.

"Where's your cassette player?" I asked him.

He looked blank a second, then smiled.

"You remember that, huh."

"How could I forget. You had me humming Misty for a week after I got home."

He laughed. "Never thought it went too good here. Besides, no time. Stick close to me or you'll get lost."

He drove smoothly, winding through the traffic, and I tried to keep tight to him. Even when other vehicles came between us it was easy to keep the big car in sight. We worked across town and headed down into the Queens-Midtown tunnel. Once through, Jimmy started making some intricate maneuvers. In ten minutes I had no idea where we were. We cut through a couple of residential areas, crossed main roads, then after a time, emerged back on a highway again. We ran that main artery awhile. Suddenly, Jimmy took a left at a major intersection, yanked his car in a quick U-turn ahead of oncoming traffic. I just made it. We went maybe two-hundred yards back in the direction from which we'd come. Then he pulled off into a crowded parking lot. There was only one old-fashioned neon tube sign over the entranceway to the restaurant. The building was low and broad. Inside it was a lot bigger than you'd think.

Things moved smoothly when we were inside. The maitre d' greeted Jimmy warmly, bringing us to a table without having to check his book. There was one large room. A lot of the tables were arranged close against the walls, with fewer than you'd expect scattered in room center. Ours was not one of the wall settings but it was far in back, close to a long, low counter. Behind the counter was a glass case with displays of seafood on crushed ice. Jimmy sat with his back toward it, facing the way we had come in. I was on his left. The waiters were slick, dark-haired young men in white jackets. We ordered drinks and Jimmy looked at me.

"You like anything special?" he asked.

"You said it's the best; most anything if that's true."

"Seafood?"

"Sure."

"Any pasta? Antipasto? Stuffed Clams? Mushrooms?"

"Great."

"Why don't you let me order a variety of stuff. I know them pretty good here."

I agreed. He looked awfully serious to be enjoying dinner. He held an intense conversation with our waiter in Italian, and there was a lot of hand-talk to help it along. He was like a general before the launch of a major campaign.

"When we're done, I'll tell you how to go back the direct route; not like we came."

"Good. How's Doc?"

That loosened him up a little. He told me Ed was fine, but that the pressures of the hospital were starting to get to Doc again. The antipasto came, the crab-stuffed mushrooms, and then a small dish of mussels in rich red sauce. It was all wonderful, and I told him.

"It better be," Jimmy said. "They got a clientele that'd let them know if it wasn't. You know who's here — right now?"

I didn't. I also did not look obviously around the low-key, smoothly running restaurant to see. Jimmy told me. He started at the wall tables to my left as I was facing them, ticking off the names, then moving to the tables on the wall behind me, never glancing in either direction. It was some display of peripheral vision, or maybe total recall of an instant mental record he'd made when we came in. If there was a Mafia social directory, his list would have filled several pages. The squid came next.

Jimmy ate with the same intensity he had given our order. When a dish came he worked through it steadily, not stopping until it was gone. His color was still bad and I could see the perspiration on his forehead. But he murmured appreciatively over the food. There were some awkward stalls in our conversation, and I tried to steer the talk back to our trip, back to fishing. He hadn't forgotten.

We talked about the two camps, the little trout river in the sun, and of course his big char. He brought up the episodes we'd shared, and I could see all of it would always be with him.

Jimmy remembered his trouble early in our trip trying to get the red char to hit. He told me how he worried that he'd never even get a big fish on — just to feel it pull one time. And over everything it was his fight with the big char that stayed.

"You know, Father Flanagan, near the end I was really beat. I mean I didn't know about holding on any more. But I figured that fish had to be pretty whipped, too. Well, I figured even with what little bit of working ticker I got left I'd just take it steady and slow and use my shoulders to pump and swing, because my arms were getting pretty dead. And — I didn't tell Doc — the old shiv was starting to turn right here." He gently tapped his chest with a balled fist. "I'll tell you besides that I was sure them little hooks would go — bend or just pull right out. But they held up didn't they. That's still my favorite lure. I got it hanging in that char's mouth back home. I got it in the living room so you can't miss it when you come in. My wife don't mind. Some fish." he said.

He looked at me, happily, but then it started to go and things slipped back. You could see it around the edges. What came was the look of wariness with a little bit of anger. And that was what stayed during the rest of the meal. It was there when we went out into the parking lot where he gave me very detailed instructions for getting back using the main roads, avoiding a couple of choice neighborhoods.

"So, you heading straight back home?" I asked.

"In a little bit. I got a little business to tie up here first."

He held the open window frame of my car as though not quite ready to let go.

"Maybe you can come over to my place sometime and see the char."

"I'd like to."

"Maybe it'll work out."

He straightened up, patted the window frame once. "So go; get the hell out of here."

"See you," I said.

He just waved, stepping back two steps. I swung out on the highway and saw him in the rear-view mirror with his arm still raised. Then the night traffic closed in from behind.

F̲our weeks passed before Jimmy's wife called to let me know that he was dead. They had taken him to the hospital but there was nothing left to work with and he wanted to go home. The first thing I thought about was that he never got to use the guest room in Doc's vacation house.

"I moved his fish into the bedroom where he was," she told me. She had a soft, kind voice, a little husky.

"He had a blowup of that one picture you sent him of

himself and Ed and the big fish. I put it right next to his bed, and the fish was on the wall right in front of him. I just thought you might want to know, and I wanted to ask you if you had any other pictures of him from his big trip."

I had pictures. Some were the kind I could send her.

"I think he went happy," she said. "He's probably the only one from his lousy high-school class that went happy." She stopped a moment. "It's pretty empty around here. He really filled the place. You always knew when he was around."

"I know."

"Did you get to know him pretty good, then?" she asked.

"I'm not sure," I said.

Market Price

At high slack tide, the old Ford pickup's single headlamp beam probed between the dunes, then caught the surf once, as the vehicle turned to run parallel with the ocean. The cone of light settled to an irregular flickering bounce aimed down the midnight beach. The high water forced the four-wheel-drive truck to wallow in soft tracks above the high-water mark. It ran canted sharply to one side from the slope of the beach. Nothing but a full-size rig would have held the three young men squeezed inside the cab.

Peer Björnson drove. It was his truck. Covering the passenger door with well over 200 pounds of bulk was BJ Cavendish. Sandwiched between them sat Spiderman Hooper, he of the carrot-colored hair and never-tan skin that looked pale even in darkness — perhaps in response to the terrifying thought of the vehicle rolling and coming to a stop with BJ's side up.

To Peer Björnson's left the low surf rolled endlessly beneath an almost full moon. It was nearly bright enough to drive without the headlight, and Peer planned to douse it when they drew a little closer to the place where they would again set up. They each wore wet waders that rubbed stiffly against one another on the hard bounces. Otherwise there was just the sound of the engine and the sea. It was late summer. Down East.

"I sure hope we do some business," Spiderman said suddenly.

"Ought to," BJ told him. "That bar's had a nice rip lately. Nature Boy took three good fish a couple days back." He began to hum dissonantly in his deep rumbly voice.

"What'd Nature Boy do yesterday?" Peer asked. There was a little rock ledging up ahead, jutting from the sand, and he pulled the wheel over, knocking out BJ's final note straight from the diaphragm.

"Don't ask," BJ said.

"Big bass or lots?"

"Just two. One of 'em went fifty." He shook his head.

"Guy gets the breaks. But he works for them," Peer said.

"I don't know how he goes so long with no sleep — every night all alone, him and that little chi-dog."

BJ rumpled thick fingers through his shaggy dark hair. "Maybe he gets some shut-eye by day on the job."

Suddenly, Spiderman cut them off sharply, jabbing a hand into the windshield. "Hey — look at . . . what the hell *is* that?"

The other two saw it as he spoke, Peer popping his foot from the accelerator just for a moment. The thing was up ahead at the diffused edge of the headlight beam. It had been illuminated as the truck lurched briefly toward the ocean.

There was another rock ledge in the beach jutting from the slope just below them and the high-water mark. The white surging push of water flooded up and over it before retreating frantically to meet the next wave. The dark shape lay upon the ledge in shadow.

"Jeezum, somebody musta drowned," said the Spiderman.

"No," Peer said softly. He gunned the engine and the truck spun sand, then churned forward. Forty feet their side of the ledge, he yanked the wheel, turning the truck briefly upslope, then hard over, swinging them down, bringing the headlamp directly on target. They were out and running.

They ran in the headlight's glare, clumsy in waders, sending long shadows ahead of them down the white, bubbly surf that surged and ebbed over the ledge, hissed and broke around the dark, silvery shape.

"Holy mother . . ." BJ began. Spiderman's high tenor knifed him short.

"Tuna! Oh, God, a whole tunafish!"

The fish lay with its head angled slightly up the beach slope, its great disk eye that in life could radiate with almost human light now horribly flat, a giant lifeless doll's eye.

Peer was first to the fish, walking in the shin-deep water around the cobalt back of the tuna, circling around to the silvery underbelly. He placed his hand on a flank.

"It'll go about six or seven hundred," he said. "I wonder what happened."

"Maybe came out of a net," BJ said. "Or maybe fought to death by some sport who lost him or let him go without helping him come around." He patted the fish. It made the same sound as slapping a side of skinned beef.

"If he's in so good shape we should get top bucks for him," said the Spiderman. "Can we get him in the truck?"

"I don't know," Peer told him. "I'll try it." He left the fish, walked back to the truck and yelled to them. "Hey, you guys give me a hand taking all this stuff out."

They hurried back and began unloading the fishing gear from the truck bed. They made a single pile in the sand above high water. Then Peer turned the truck completely around. He backed the old, blue Ford down beside the fish on the ledge. Surf washed around the wheel rims.

"How do you think we're going to do this?" BJ asked. He sloshed to the fish, put a shoulder to it and heaved. The tail and hindquarters rocked. That was all.

"I have some line," Peer said, "and the comealong." He took the rope and the handwinch from behind the seat, threw the line to Spiderman and got up into the bed. "Tie around the tail," he said.

With the line lashed just forward of the tuna's tail, Spiderman walked back to the truck and handed the rope up. Peer looked for a place to anchor the comealong's hook, finally dropped it over the front edge of the bed. He slipped a bowline loop over the hook at the other end of the comealong. "Here, you get up and work this, I'm heavier," he said to Spiderman. He dropped down into the lapping water.

"We can maybe turn it first," BJ offered.

They went to the foresection of the big tuna, waited until the ratcheting click of the comealong started, then as the line came drum tight, began to heave their combined weight against the carcass. Slowly the tuna turned, pivoting on the ledge, angling its tail end toward the open bed.

"Wait," Peer said. He went to the truck again, took some tools from behind the seat. "If we get anywhere, I got to take the tailgait off or it'll bend right down." He handed BJ the flashlight from the tool kit. The bolts were rusted, and it took a little while, but they finally freed the gate. BJ carried it back to the other equipment up the beach.

BJ tossed the flashlight back in the truck and returned with Peer to the fish. The line was still taut when Spiderman started cranking the comealong again. They could hear the ratchet over the sound of the ocean. In unison, they strained against the tuna's side, trying to rock it to start it sliding. Then the great fish inched forward. It moved again until the tail section cleared the edge of the bed.

"You think this line will take it?" BJ said.

"I don't think so," Peer said. They were both panting.

The comealong clicked again. Suddenly Spiderman yelled.

"Hold it, hold it! Jeeze, the truck's breaking."

They ran to him. In the moonlight they could see that the entire front section of the bed was bending in, and where the comealong hook was fastened, the metal had crumpled into a V.

"You know how to release that?" Peer asked.

"Yeah, but I need the light," Spiderman told him. Peer got it. Spiderman found and pressed the release lever, then cranked the comealong in reverse. The hind section of the fish slowly sagged from the end of the bed.

Peer shook his head. "We'll have to wait," he said. "Wait until the tide goes down. Then I can drive below that ledge."

"Just drop it off into the truck?" BJ said. "Man, do you think it'll hold — I mean the truck."

"How old's this truck?" Spiderman asked.

"Pretty old," Peer said. "It's been a good old truck, too. But I've carried that much weight before, I think."

"Well, I guess we'll wait," said BJ.

They unfastened the line from the fish. Peer pulled the pickup back up to dry sand, and they sat in their waders facing the ocean, the tuna pale in the moonlight.

"It's a lot of bucks lying there," Spiderman said. "What were they getting — up to seven like this?"

"Not here. I think more like four in the round if you're lucky," BJ said. "Still, you figure, if it goes seven hundred . . ."

"What's going to happen is it's going to go down again, eventually," Peer said. "The Japanese figured out this new super-quick-freeze system. They say you can't tell it from the fresh. And that's even for sashimi. They stockpile enough, the price is going to come down."

"That's where the big bucks are; for that raw fish," Spiderman said.

"They always paid best in fall, though," said BJ.

"Fish from the Maritimes," Peer said. "They're fattest, and in the best shape in fall. That's when they paid the top dollar."

The ocean crept back slowly. It left the ledge, first lapping the underside of the rock formation as it went, then foaming and hissing on the sand below. It backed its way down the gentle slope, leaving the sand wet and smooth, pocked here and there with pebbles and an occasional shell fragment. From time to time, one of them got up to check the progress of the retreat. On his last look, BJ called back to them.

"I think we might have it. You ought to come look."

They joined him below the ledge. There was a fairly wide strip of wet sand there now, and Peer walked on it, testing its hardness with his boots. Spent waves of the receding tide rolled against the shore, sending little fingers of foam that no longer reached them, hurrying up the beach.

Peer sighed. "Well, we better try it, I guess." He started the truck, brought it down the beach onto the fresh, wet hard-packed sand and continued down below the ledge where the tuna lay. They positioned the truck bed just below the fish, lengthwise, giving it the best chance for catching the carcass. Peer got out and checked, then climbed up to the ledge.

"Let's go for it," BJ rumbled. They dug their feet against the ledge and thrust their combined weight against the fish. "Rock it," BJ yelled. "Like a car. Heave. Heave. Heave . . ."

The tuna rocked in place. It inched forward a little on the rock, then stalled on an insignificant looking knob.

Panting for breath, Peer called a halt. He went back to the truck and took out a high-lift jack and a board kept for freeing mired beach vehicles. He planted the board like a lever in the space between the fish and the rock knob and had Spiderman start to jack. They slammed their shoulders into the fish, beginning the rhythmic rocking once again. The tuna slid over the small projection. Very slowly, it worked to the edge of the outcropping.

"Keep it going, we're getting it!" BJ yelled, "Heave . . ."

One moment their shoulders were mashed to unyielding solidness, the next, it was gone. The fish dropped so suddenly, they fell to their knees. The fish slammed the truck with a metallic clanging, a sound of ripping, breaking things. The pickup bottomed on its suspension, wrenched dangerously over, then the tuna ripped out the entire side of the bed as it rolled to the sand.

The truck righted itself but still listed to one side.

"Oh, no," Spiderman wailed.

Except for the surf, it was very quiet.

They walked down to the truck. Not only was the side of the bed gone, the place where the fish had hit was dished in and torn open. They could see the frame through the vent in the rusty metal.

"Damn." Peer said. He went to the torn side and pulled at it. It was still attached by a small piece to the bed's front.

"Here, let me," BJ said. He walked the panel around like a swinging gate, moved it back and forth several times. The fatigued metal gave way completely. He threw the panel back into what was left of the bed.

"We're going to have that mother," Peer said. He walked up the beach to the equipment pile, returning with the rope. He doubled it, handing the loose ends to Spiderman, then crawled beneath the truck to tie the looped section to the frame of the pickup. "Tie that to the tail, again," he called out to Spiderman. He rolled out, dusting sand from his shirt. "Help me get all that other gear back in this thing," he said. They loaded the partially destroyed truck, Peer weaving another piece of line around everything to keep it from falling out where the side had been.

"There's that access to the road just about forty yards up the beach," Peer said. "If I can get that fish moving I won't stop. Just jump in someplace."

He got in the truck which started immediately, He put it in gear and came tight, gently, against the doubled line. Then he revved the engine and slipped out the clutch. The truck settled, as though hunkering down to jump. The tires caught, slipped, dug small depressions in the sand, then caught again. The truck began moving slowly forward, and the tunafish followed it. BJ and the Spiderman cheered.

The tide was further out now, and Peer swung toward the water, coming 180 degrees about. The fish skidded on the wet sand. With the gained momentum Peer angled the truck up the slope. Spiderman leaped into the broken bed, and BJ flung himself inside the cab. The truck increased speed on the hardpack. They headed down the beach, and when they had nearly reached the access, Peer turned directly for it. They slowed when they hit the soft, dry sand, but did not stall.

"Man I hope we don't skin the thing like this," BJ said. Peer gripped the wheel, jaw clenched, eyes riveted ahead, downshifting once, the truck rocking and jolting. They reached the paved road, swung out, and parked the fish neatly on the shoulder.

"All right!" hollered Spiderman from the back.

"Now what?" said BJ.

The truck was pulled ahead of the fish on the road shoulder. Peer poked his head out the window, his straight blond hair hanging in disarray. He looked at the sky to the east, which had become pink and yellow with little bean-shaped purple clouds scudding high.

"Somebody's got to stay with the fish," Peer said. "I'm going into town for my brother."

"What's up?" Spiderman said. He had come around to the driver's window.

"I'm going to get Kurt to open the grocery store."

"How's that going to help?" BJ asked.

"Dollies. And I'll get more tow rope."

BJ raised his eyes to the sky, understanding.

"We're going to roll this fish back to town and all the way to Placket's, where they can weigh it and lay some serious bucks on us. Just like a giant skateboard," Peer said.

"I'll stay with the fish," Spiderman offered.

"I'll go," said BJ. "Help you off-load all that tackle."

Spiderman crawled under the truck and untied the towline. They looked back at the fish, which was gray and dusty, a patina of sand blown over it.

"Keep the flies and poachers off," Peer said. He started down the road, the pickup heeling so far over on the wrecked side it seemed likely that it might turn over.

It was mid-morning when they returned. The square, wood-frame dollies with metal wheels were stacked in the broken bed. There was new line and two crowbars. They went to work with little conversation, grunting, prying at the carcass. Peer used the jack, as well. Finally the dollies were in place, staggered along the length of the fish from its head to just forward of the tail section. Spiderman lashed the new rope again around the peduncle ahead of the tail. They rigged another line through the mouth and gills and brought the high good side of the pickup alongside the fish. They rigged the lines like a boat's bow and stern lines to the front bumper support and the rear frame of the truck. Spiderman climbed into the bed.

"I think it'll work," BJ said. They started.

Peer slowly moved the truck onto the blacktop, and the great fish followed, riding alongside and slightly to the rear.

"It's looking good," Spiderman yelled.

The dolly wheels rattled on the paving. The truck picked up speed, the dollies rumbling like an elevated train going by. Spiderman looked over carefully and saw the sparks coming now and then from the steel wheels.

They sat tensely, willing nothing to go wrong. Peer gripped the steering wheel hard enough to turn his knuckles white. Then BJ snapped on the radio. It played loudly, a song in a high-pitched country-western whine.

"Yee-hah," hollered Spiderman from the back.

A gray cloudbank moved across the morning sky as they came to the edge of town. Peer kept to the side and back streets as much as possible, but he stopped everyone. On the sidewalks people stopped to stare. They came from doorways, hung from windows. One rubbernecker in a car slammed into the rear of another car at a traffic light. Both drivers left their vehicles to watch the procession.

There was only one stretch left before they would reach the fish buyer on the wharf. Only one stretch, but it was down the main street of town, which, at midday, would be crowded with people.

At the end of the side street they were on there was a traffic light. It was green.

"Let's get it over with," Peer said gritting his teeth. He touched the accelerator, aiming for the corner. He was a tad too fast.

They started into the turn too quickly. Peer hit the brakes once but kept the truck's turn arc smooth. It was a right-hand turn, and Peer had just completed it when, from the corner of his eye, he saw the tuna coming. The fish came like a water ski tuber in a pendulum swing following a speedboat playing crack-the-whip. It swung in an accelerating arc, and he felt the rear end of the truck lurch once as the stern line hit and snapped. He saw the tuna passing, shooting straight down Main Street, saw the open black Mercedes convertible with the pretty blonde lady driver about 80 feet down the oncoming lane, the direction in which the fish was heading. Peer stood on the brake pedal. The great fish on its wheeled dollies came to the end of the bow line and snapped the rope.

The final restraint on the line before it broke had changed the fish's direction. Instead of heading for the black Mercedes, the tuna now rumbled directly for the wheeled cart of a street vendor. On the cart were running shoes, sandals and a potpourri of brightly hued T-shirts. Those in line of the fish's travel leaped aside. Peer had a fleeting view of the street vendor's look of horror as he left his inventory to its fate and jumped over a folding wood chair out of the way.

The fish hit the right side of the target. The cart spun, then flipped, sending its wares high into the air, scattering across the sidewalk and street. The fish continued on, coming to rest in the open doorway of a restaurant, between two outside seating areas. A waitress dropped her tray from shoulder height. Somewhere a dog began barking madly. An airborne green T-shirt dropped over the head of the fish.

Then the street became a bedlam of shouts. The three jumped from the truck, running toward the fish. The vendor waved his arms, screaming. Peer and BJ were at the cart, trying to right it. Spiderman plucked the T-shirt from the tuna. The lettering on its front read "Save the Whales."

"You crazy, you guys?" shouted the vendor. "Whatta you think you're doing? Whatta you gonna *do* about this?"

"Sorry. Sorry." BJ said.

"Don't worry, we'll take care of you, we'll pay you for this," Peer tried soothingly.

They got the cart back on its wheels. Peer dug for his wallet. "Here. Hey you guys, help me out with this." The other two fumbled for some bills. They thrust the money in the vendor's hand. He stopped shouting. The owner of the restaurant had not.

"You idiots get this thing outta here!" he hollered.

Peer pulled the truck up to the restaurant, where people nearest the fish were leaving quickly. A few men in the crowd came over to help. Traffic was still at a standstill. They began shoving the fish back onto the street. The lines were still attached to the tuna. They rolled the fish back to the down-listing side of the truck. Peer fastened the forward line to the pulled-up bumper while Spiderman and BJ worked on the stern line.

Peer saw a policeman walking toward them. "Let's get out of here," he yelled at the others.

They hurried back into the truck and started down the street, the crowd parting, still noisy, the vendor gathering up his shoes and shirts, the restauranteur standing, hands on hips, shaking his head. They moved at a subdued pace along Main Street with the tuna rolling smoothly alongside, both tourists and locals gawking as they passed.

"That cop stayed back there. He's not coming," Spiderman called to them from the truck bed.

They were past the main shopping areas, at the place where the street angled down to the wharf where both commercial and private sportfishermen unloaded, sold fish, gassed, iced and resupplied with bait.

Peer pulled the truck alongside the back of Placket's wholesalers. They hurried from the truck. "Let's get these lines off and move the truck away," Peer said. "It just looks pretty weird. I'm going to try to find a hose or bucket anyway to wet the fish off." He looked at the tuna. It lay stiff and dusty on the dollies.

"It could look better," BJ said.

The lines free, Spiderman backed the truck away, parked it and rejoined BJ. It was busy at the front side of the old, peeling, wood-frame building. There were scales, chain falls for weighing and winching big fish. Inside the building were freezers and refrigerators, cleaning and boxing facilities. Peer came back with two buckets of water. They wet down the fish, and it returned to some semblance of presentability.

"Let's go find somebody," Peer said.

"I'm not moving from the fish," Spiderman said.

BJ and Peer went around front. The dealer was just finishing with a boat. "What do you fellas have?" he asked.

"One bluefin. Maybe close to seven hundred," BJ said.

"Great," said the dealer. "Where you tied up?"

"We're not," Peer told him. "The fish's around back."

"Back? How'd it get there?"

"Better you didn't ask," BJ told him.

"I got to see this," the dealer said.

They went around back. The dealer stopped. Spiderman waved to him in greeting. "I'm *not* going to ask," said the dealer. "Any of you know how to run . . . no, never mind."

He went around front and yelled inside the building. "Hey Walt, you wanna give me a hand here."

Walt came out. He was a very large gentleman, pushing six-three, maybe two-thirty. He was not fat.

"Listen," the dealer said to him. "It's been a long day, so I'm not going to explain. I don't think I could anyway. We got a bluefin out back on some dollies. Either you and these guys who brought it can try to roll it around here or go down to Davie's and borrow the fork lift to get it in."

Walt looked at him. "Let's go see," he said.

They opted for a roll, with Walt's extra bulk and obvious strength. The fish did not object. It came along cooperatively.

Walt got the chainfall down, rope-wrapped the tail and hooked into the stout line. They winched the fish high, Peer trying to keep its best side toward the dealer. Walt went back inside.

The fish weighed 678 pounds.

"Look," said the dealer, "I don't know about this fish. There are a couple of Japanese buyers here now. I'd like to give you top buck, but only if I get high dollar, too. Well, we'll see. Let me make a quick call."

He went in and they waited. Then BJ said, "I could use a beer."

"Anything," said Spiderman. "All my cash is gone. I gave it for that T-shirt guy."

"You didn't have much on you, then." BJ said. "I think I saw what you kicked in."

Spiderman was about to reply when a dark-haired man in tie and sport jacket climbed from one of the large sportfishing boats and walked up. He had a slim folding briefcase beneath his arm. He smiled at the three.

"Hello boys," he said.

They nodded, greeting him noncommittally.

"Turned out a nice one after all, eh? Your fish?"

"Yes," Peer told him.

"How heavy?"

"Six-seventy-eight of prime tunafish," Spiderman said.

"You a buyer?"

The man in the jacket smiled. "No, not a buyer," he said.

Just then the dealer came out. He saw the dark-haired man at once. "Well I think we can do you pretty good, boys," he said. "You might as well give him your permit information, then I'll get it for my records. I'll bring this fish inside while you're doing that."

"Permit?" BJ said. He looked at Peer, who looked at Spiderman. They looked at the man with the briefcase.

"Your fishing permit," said the man. "One fish per boat per day. Per permit."

"Well who are you with?" Peer said.

"National Marine Fisheries Service," said the dark-haired man. He began opening his case.

"Federal, huh," said Spiderman.

"Uh, we weren't exactly fishing," BJ said.

The federal man had pulled out a report form. In its title they could clearly see the word "violation."

"Harpooning, then?" said the Fisheries man.

"No," said Spiderman. "Look, it was really sort of a . . . *gift.*"

"Sure," Peer said. "C'mon downstreet with us, first, there's a T-shirt guy there who can start to tell you about it."

The federal man took out a pen. It was quiet enough to hear the click as he pushed the point forward. "Sorry, boys," was all he said.

At The End Of The River

It was three weeks since the last rain, and the big river was dropping two or three inches every day. Still, the fish continued to come. Each day, fresh runs of Atlantic salmon swam from the vastness of the gulf into a bewildering constriction of nets at the mouth of the river. Those that escaped entered the twisting channels of the delta, then passed into an aquatic steeplechase of waterfalls that grew ever higher going inland. Between the falls were patches of quiet water a mile or longer.

With the low water, the first fish to have entered the river were now locked below the steepest falls. Downstream, salmon continued to fight over the lesser cataracts, though each day fewer of them were succeeding.

At the mouth of the river, four men in chest waders walked along a short headland jutting into the troubled green-brown water flowing out to sea. At the point of the headland they faced into the wind that had come in the night, and looked out over the seething gulf. Roller after breaker of hissing waves beat toward the river mouth.

"Glad we don't have to go into *that*," said Ed Nickerson, a slender red-haired man whose waders seemed far too large for him.

Jim Ritter, the big angler next to him, waved an arm slightly upriver. His deep, resonant voice carried well above the wind. "It doesn't look any too friendly right here, either," he said.

"We won't get out of it soon," said Roger Hudson. His angular frame was bent into the wind for a moment more, then he turned impatiently to go. "I don't know if we'll get out of it up by the falls, either."

The fourth angler, Jeff Perry, said nothing. As the assigned trip photographer, he was busy trying to shoot the view of the churning water with the others in the foreground, but everyone kept shifting. Finally, he settled for Nickerson, who alone stood in place, staring in perverse fascination at the violent scene before him.

"Got it," Perry said finally, then, out from behind the viewfinder, looked more closely at the river mouth, squinting gray-blue eyes in the wind. "God, it really is rough," he murmured.

They slid down the slope of the headland and walked to the beach of the little cove where commercial fishing craft and a few skiffs bobbed at their moorings. The two Indians they had hired to take them up to the camp waters to fish stood in hip boots, holding their ancient skiffs. In the middle of the river the anglers could see the long exposed sand bars and what seemed to be a low ribbon of mist hanging over them. The men waded out, Roger Hudson faster than the others, already climbing with his tackle into the first skiff. Big

Jim Ritter was next, dropping equipment into the second boat. He got in and Nickerson joined him, leaving Jeff Perry to pile his mound of photographic equipment as well as tackle in Hudson's boat.

The skiffs were ragged things with gouges and breaks in the gel coat. They were old modified gullwing hulls and they were powered by 20-horsepower engines that had been worked very hard. Norman, the Indian boatman of the skiff Perry and Hudson rode, swung his shoulders easily against the starter cord, coaxing the engine to life. When it caught, he turned, dropped to the rear seat and twisted the throttle full open. In seconds they were out of the lee of the headland, and the wind coming up the river hit them hard. They met the waves at full bore, pounding from their seats and slamming down violently again. The engine ran with an ear-splitting howl, far louder than a 20-horse outboard had any right to sound.

Norman glanced over his shoulder into the wind. His companion's boat, which had closed considerably, was aground. He turned ahead with indifference, and they boomed ahead into the chop, the anglers grabbing the flat cushionless seats, trying to ease the blows jarring their spines.

In the other skiff, Nickerson was on his feet the moment they ground to a halt. Now he stared into the water while in the stern the moon-faced boatman jabbed angrily at the bottom with his oar.

"We're at the end of a little bar," Nickerson said. "You can see the grass on the bottom, even with this water so colored up. I don't think it's more than seven inches deep."

Ritter nodded. He looked at the Indian. "What's your name?," he asked. The man patted his chest once.

"Michael," he said. He smiled.

"Michael, you want us out of the boat? Push?" Ritter asked.

The Indian shook his head, motioned with his hand

palm down, obviously meaning for them to stay. It took only a few minutes for him to push off the bar.

Michael yanked the starter cord. The engine caught, and he jammed it into gear. Nickerson just dropped in time. "What is this, some kind of race — who gets there first?" he yelled over the howling engine.

Ritter shrugged, shook his head. His hat had been knocked off, and his fine dark hair blew in the wind as he groped to find it.

They went aground twice more before the country along the banks began to change. From low, marshy delta, they entered slightly higher bottomland, then a stretch of high sand cliffs topped with low vegetation. In scattered places along the cliffs, ground water oozed through, trickling down to the river, staining the light sand ocher or rust where the rivulets ran. And then the sand banks gave way to rock and the scrub trees became tall spruce, hemlock or cedar broken with birch and aspen. They rounded a sharp bend and saw the other boat pulled up on a low, flat granite ledge.

Michael nudged his boat into a little cut in the rocks next to Norman's skiff. They hiked up a trail into the woods, leaving the two boatmen to wait for their return at the end of the day. Above the first falls in a small cove was a broad aluminum boat in which sat an old, nearly toothless Indian guide who would take them to their fishing beats below the next set of falls. The run was twenty minutes up the lakelike steady in the shelter of forest stands covering high shores. Then the banks thrust back suddenly from the great drop of the next falls. Huge gray granite shoulders where the river fell and pounded were without trees for some distance back from the river. The wind found them again.

The old man motored directly to a point at the base of the falls. He nudged his bow into a little hollow in the rocks in quiet water, motioning for two of the anglers to get out.

"Fish right here?" Roger Hudson asked, indicating the side currents and slower runs.

The guide nodded, pointed farther out, sweeping his arm around in a wide semicircle, indicating the whole area was good.

Perry followed Hudson, hauling his camera bag and tackle.

"You're going to have a helluva time casting," Ritter pointed. "You've got to throw right into the wind here."

"Well, we'll switch off later. Get the guide to pick us up in a few hours and we'll trade places," Hudson said. He was climbing up the rocks, pulling line from his reel to cast. And then in the white water out in strong current, two salmon leaped. One of them made it up a level of the tiered falls. The other was thrown back. They all saw it.

The old guide took Ritter and Nickerson down river again where a steep-shored rock arm elbowed from shore, cleaving the current. Thirty yards down the arm the guide cut in and came around facing into the current, running the bow gently between tumbled boulders. The two anglers stepped out. There was only a narrow ledge on which to stand. They climbed the steep, black rock and began picking their ways to the point where they would fish.

Once there, Nickerson cut to the right, dropping closer to the water. They would have to fish from exposed and narrow ledges. Ritter's perch was high and he could see well down into the water, which was clear and tinted the color of strong tea. Near shore there were two submerged boulders, and farther out a great ledge formed by an underwater extension of the point on which he stood. The wind was at his back. He flicked his fly line into the air, letting the wind catch it. Suddenly the current smoothed and he could see through the water just off the outermost boulder, the long, lovely shapes of three salmon showing light against the bottom.

"Hey," he called to Nickerson. "Salmon here."

"Tell me about it!" shouted Nickerson over the wind. "I've already had two rises. Nothing took."

Ritter's first cast was slightly off. He let the fly drift past the lie, stripped off more line than was necessary. On his second cast the wind took the fly line from his open left hand before he could control it, and the tightly clipped bomber with its gaudy orange hackles flew much farther than he wanted. He swore softly.

He let the bug drift lightly on the surface. It was far enough out so its drift would be along the deep side of the ledge that had been visible when the water smoothed. Suddenly he saw the fish. It was not of the group of three lying by the boulder. This salmon came from deeper water. It was a huge fish, slightly colored. He could see it clearly, turning now, coming up behind the fly, following it.

"Take it, take it, oh, take it . . ." Ritter pleaded, slipping line to keep the drift going. He felt his heart pounding in his temples. The bomber drifted beautifully and the salmon followed it, nose inches away, closing on it, finally touching, bumping the high floater. Ritter saw the bomber jump.

"Oh, God!" he said, but did not snap the fly away. He saw the great fish sinking now, fading, dropping away from the surface. He felt himself shaking slightly. He lifted the fly from the water for another cast, changed his mind, and pulled it short. He yelled over to Nickerson, telling him what had happened.

"I had fish come twice," Nickerson called back. "No touching the fly, though. Went through three patterns. Now I'm back to the first. They're moving but they won't take. I'm shaking like an amateur."

"Maybe it's the low water. Temperature's got to be high," Ritter said.

"Who knows."

They took no fish. Before they switched beats, Jeff Perry hooked up once at the falls but the fish was lost. The day was more than over. Going down in the old guide's boat, Roger Hudson looked at his watch.

"We're a little late," he said. "I hope our guys didn't decide to take off."

"I'd almost forgotten about that little joy ride," Nickerson said. "How I look forward to it."

"We're more than a little late," Ritter said. "Considering how long it took us to get here, I figure it'll be dark just about when we're starting into the lower river maze."

"Ah, they know the river," Hudson said.

"Maybe your guy."

"Well, we'll stay together."

"If you can convince them. They got some kind of leg-up thing going with each other," Nickerson said.

The two Indian boatmen who had brought them up the river waited by their skiffs. The moon-faced Michael paced along a small outcropping while Norman lounged on his side in a small depression in the rock out of the wind, looking cat comfortable. They went to their boats as soon as they saw the anglers coming.

The four automatically headed for the skiffs in which they had come. Norman shoved his boat out, holding the bow into the current.

Michael looked at Ritter and Nickerson. "Salmon?" he queried.

"No salmon," Ritter told him.

Passing Michael's skiff, Hudson saw the black plastic trash bag in the bottom of the boat, its mouth folded back and held shut by the weight of the long objects within it.

"Salmon?" he asked the Indian.

The boatman nodded.

"Let's see."

"OK," Michael said. He stood between the anglers and

his skiff, fussed a moment before turning with a slightly colored male fish in his arms. The fish was an easy 15 pounds.

"Nice," Hudson told him. "OK, let's go."

He turned to Nickerson and Ritter, speaking so they could just hear over the sound of the river.

"I don't think his salmon ate the fly," he said. "Probably snagged, the way they were stacked in at the base of these falls and not hitting."

Perry was fussing with his camera gear in Norman's boat. "If you guys are worried about being late, let's get going," he said.

They did — and Ritter had been right. Dusk was darkening into night when they rounded the last bend that separated the true river from the lower estuary. The wind pummeled them, stronger than it had been that morning. As before, it carried bolts of slashing sand, but now they were running full into it. There was one other small gift.

When they hit the open water, both boatman standing at their tillers were almost knocked from their feet. The skiffs reared suddenly, then slammed on the surface, now an endless expanse of jagged peaks and seething valleys.

In the skiff he rode, Perry lunged for his camera bag. "What in hell . . ." he started.

Even Norman, obviously the more experienced of the two boatmen, floundered for a moment. He quickly gained his balance, grinned at his passengers and waved at the water.

"Tide change," he informed them.

"It's going out!" Hudson yelled. "Right into the wind."

Still they did not slow. There was no position, no location the anglers could find to help absorb the vicious slamming.

For a moment the two skiffs drew near one another. In Norman's boat, Perry was lying forward, his weight helping to hold down the bow. Michael slowed, motioning to Ritter to take a similar location. It was all right sliding forward, but when they throttled up again, Ritter thought perhaps he would be knocked unconscious. He saw for a moment his friends in the other skiff, their heads whipping like those of rag dolls, like the dummies used in automobile crash simulations. He tried to lie on his side in the bow, and finding that impossible, rolled around on his haunches to a kind of hunkering position. The pounding was disproportionately worse up forward without some boat length to absorb shock. He thought his vertebrae might splinter. Nickerson had slipped from the center seat and was crouching on hands and knees on the deck like an animal at bay. Each rearing of the skiff lifted him into the air and when he dropped it was to the deck flying up to meet him. His knees were taking the full shock of it. He tried rolling on one buttock, and held there a little while.

Spray, then waves sloshed over the gunwales and began accumulating in the bottom of the boat. The two salmon slid partially from their plastic shroud, working back and forth in sandy grit and water. Nickerson saw their heads in the failing light, watched their lazy sliding appearance and retreat into the sack. Then pain in his hip bored through, forcing him to react. He knew his knees could take no more hammering, and he pushed himself back on the seat and leaned forward, trying to raise himself with hands and arms when the skiff hit an especially high wave.

The boatmen had slowed, but the tops of the waves continued to sheer along the sides of the skiff and slop in. Michael ran his boat in a half crouch, one knee on the stern seat, head turning as he scanned the way ahead, illuminated now mainly by starlight. Ed saw him suddenly turn, then tug hard at something behind and below before straightening again.

In the bow, Ritter continued to roll in pain. Something fell from Nickerson's jacket pocket, and he realized it was the small, waterproof flashlight he carried. He groped for it, found it, and turned it on to see if it would still work. The high-intensity light flashed on. The beam caught Michael in the face, and he lifted his arm to shield his eyes. In the sudden shock of light, Nickerson had seen a shiny metallic ring around a finger of the boatman's upraised hand. The ring was integral with a cylindrical object, part rubber, part metal.

"Hell," Nickerson yelled over his shoulder. "He's running with the bailer open."

"What's that?" Ritter asked.

"He has the plug out to drain the boat!" Nickerson tried again.

"Good, get the water out."

If we can keep going, Nickerson thought. But what happens when we go aground on one of the sand bars? What happens when all that water surges in?

In a little while he saw the boatman bend and knew he must be putting the plug back.

Norman's boat pulled ahead of them, its silhouette disappearing around a bend of the broad estuary. Then they made the turn, and it was as though the sky had caught fire. The entire northern sky was a seething band of color. The Aurora Borealis shot great spikes of pale green and orange high into the night sky. Along the horizon, waves of rose and yellow-green undulated like the surf coming in from the gulf. The display was intense, almost violent. Then Norman's boat rammed the first sandbar.

Michael veered to the right, missing the hazard, the silhouette of the other skiff and its three occupants flickering against the glow of northern lights. Moving fast, Norman was out of the boat, wading forward to free a line from the bow. They could hear Roger yelling something. Overhead, away from the Aurora Borealis, stars glittered sharply against a black sky. The air temperature was dropping at an incredible rate.

Shortly they saw Norman's silhouette hesitate, begin to sink, then stumble back. The man struggled around and

sloshed back to his boat, away from the deepening water.
Then Michael's skiff hit hard, knocking him forward. He
caught himself, spinning the tiller too late. The Indian was
immediately over the side, walking forward in hip boots,
hand on the gunwale. He reached the bow, grabbed the line
there and began heaving on the jammed boat. Nickerson
found an oar.

"Give me one," Ritter said.

Michael moved ahead in shindeep water, the line taut
over his shoulder. Then they thought he had fallen.

The man seemed to go down on one knee as though he
had been hit from behind. He had reached a dropoff. He
struggled backwards, waving a hand at them to stop poling.
They held the skiff with the oars thrust into mud while
Michael splashed back to the skiff.

Norman's skiff roared ahead while Michael poled them
to the dropoff. Reaching it, he yanked the outboard to life as
Ritter threw tackle bags into the bow, following on top of
them. He made it just as Michael twisted open the throttle.
The skiff leaped ahead into the night. On their right the
Auroral display pulsed like a living thing.

They were making headway now, running well, and
Michael increased the boat speed. Far ahead was the silhouette of the other boat. Nickerson saw Michael pivot on
one knee to pull the plug again. Soon the skiff rode higher,
climbing on plane as water emptied from the hull. They ran
hard into the wind, and with each passing minute, their hope
and confidence built. Then without warning, the channel
ended. There was no hint in the dim light which way it
turned or branched. One moment they were running fast and
the next, the engine screamed, the prop biting air as they
struck the bar. The boatman slammed to the deck. Nickerson
was thrown forward. The bow smashed up, gear bags pounding Ritter's face. The river crashed over the transom, washed
up to the second seat, drenching the Indian and Nickerson.

Numb from the shock of collision, they saw Michael clawing upright, then begin blindly groping in the debris in the bottom of the skiff.

"Light, light!" he yelled.

Nickerson rolled painfully in the wet and confusion. He found his flashlight in a pocket, turned it on and handed it to the boatman. In the bow, Ritter was on his knees on the dunnage. Horrified, Nickerson realized what it was that Michael had lost.

The fall had knocked the plug from his finger. The skiff was on an angle, bow up on the bar, the stern in deeper water which was now bubbling in through the drain hole. The plug was gone somewhere in the chaos of equipment spilling over the bottom of the skiff. The boatman clawed the shirt bottom from his jeans while yanking his knife from its sheath on his right hip. He slashed some of the tail from his shirt, turned and jammed the end of the cloth into the drain hole. It checked the flow, but there was a lot of water in the skiff now, and the stern was very low. The other boat was gone in the night. Michael climbed over the side, reaching elbow deep into the water in the skiff bottom. In chest waders, the two anglers followed. The boatman found a rusted coffee can and began bailing with it. The other men searched through the equipment jumble for something else with which to bail. A wave that was higher than the rest crested at the skiff's stern and dropped in. Cursing, Michael bailed faster.

Ritter found a plastic container in which he stored reels, ripped it from his duffel bag and splashed aft to help the bailing effort.

"Can't find anything!" Nickerson yelled, still groping for a bailer.

"Keep trying," Ritter answered him. "We're close. Look at those lights from the village. We'll get there — if we can empty this boat."

"No, we could hardly get through in the day. Better off dragging this whole rig. Shoot straight for the village."

"We'd hit a dropoff," Ritter said. He turned his concentration to the bailing, trying to match the rapid cadence Michael had set. Their scoops scraped the skiff bottom, and the sound of water emptying heavily close to the boat was clearly audible even in the steady wind around their heads. Despite the fallen temperature they began to perspire from the effort.

The water level in the skiff dropped quickly. Soon the amount of scooped water was no longer worth the effort. Michael straightened.

"OK," he said. "Push boat."

Ritter straightened, shifted position around to the side, looking for Nickerson to be on the opposite gunwale, not seeing him, suddenly realizing he had not been bailing either, and spun around fast. Nickerson was not there.

"My God," he said into the night, then yelled his friend's name. He could hear the wind stop the sound of his voice like a heavy curtain.

"Where?" the Indian said.

"I don't know where. He's started walking." Then he yelled again. "Ed! For Godsake, Ed!"

"Pull," Michael was telling him, the boatman already heaving on the skiff. Ritter grabbed the gunwale, pulling until he thought something would burst in him. The skiff ground along the sand. They shifted their feet, braced to pull once more. The boat moved farther this time. Twice more they strained against the sucking sand and muck, and then the skiff slid free, floated lightly in the chop, no waves splashing in.

"In boat!" Michael ordered.

Ritter jammed his belly on the gunwale, rolled his legs over, fell in and scrambled forward on his hands and knees. He pointed to the lights of the village, turning to Michael.

"He must have headed for the village. Walking — village!" he yelled, jabbing his arm in the direction.

Though Ritter could not see it, the boatman nodded,

knowing. He started the engine, began motoring to the right, trying for a channel, unable to find one, feeling with the engine itself, the prop cutting against sand, then suddenly running free as they entered deeper water.

On both knees in the bow, Ritter searched the darkness ahead, straining to find a silhouette in the direction of the northern lights. Then he scanned to the left into the night. He shouted Nickerson's name into the wind until his voice broke. The wind laughed down his throat.

His certainty that the boat was lost had come clearly to Ed Nickerson. It was as obvious as the fact that there was nothing at all for him to use to help empty water from the skiff. And hadn't he spoken to Jim, told him it would be impossible to find a way, even if the boat had not been finished? And so he had struck out, moving surely, the push of water against his upper shins and knees something familiar, understandable. It was like slogging one of the little trout creeks back home, and he splashed along, striding out, feeling right about his decision, comforted by the positive action. He knew quite well where he was headed.

He was warm from the wading, and the lights of the village seemed larger and brighter. The wind bothered him even more now, beating against him with personal affront he had not felt before. The water deepened with deceptive slowness, and though it was now pressing against his thighs, Nickerson never really noticed. He slowed when the level climbed above his hips, understanding what had happened. He moved ahead gingerly, until, with the next step of his left foot, he found there was no longer any bottom. He lurched quickly back, gaining purchase again, and started off to his right, toward the Aurora Borealis.

He could see a little hump silhouette on the distance shore and headed steadily toward it after discovering that if he strayed too far to the left or right, he would begin to sink again. The long and narrow finger of bottom on which he walked began bending very slowly toward the village. Ed realized this at once, and his heart kicked excited and happy in his chest. He began forcing himself ahead faster. Then the bottom went away quite unexpectedly, and although he knew where to kick to find it again, after doing so it was not there. Water flooded into his sleeves and jacket throat. It also ran in small rivulets down his chest into his waders. He had the good wader belt cinched tightly around his waist, and not a lot of water was going to get in there, and anyway he had seen the demonstrations of anglers leaping into swimming pools and even into rivers while they were wearing chesthigh waders, and knew you were supposed to be able to float that way — even with waders full of water. But he felt himself sinking, and began to kick and to strike out with his arms, bulky in his rain jacket, as were his legs in the wide, old-fashioned, canvas-covered waders.

The kicking of his legs did not move him much, and he slowed the cadence, trying to conserve energy, but could not quit altogether or he would begin sinking. His arms produced the real forward movement. He tried a breast stroke that turned into a side stroke and scissor kick, and he tried to move back where he knew the finger of bottom had to be. He swam a good thirty feet before groping with one foot to find the vanished bottom. He turned to the right and swam again without finding a footfall, then turned 180 degrees and doubled the distance. There was no bottom. He tread water, turning slowly, scanning the surface as far as he could see into the night. He tried to find some difference in the dancing water that would indicate a shoal or flat, but the surface looked the same in all directions. And so he would have to concentrate on keeping afloat, perhaps for a long time, until the wind or current moved him into the shallows.

Suddenly he was aware of being terribly cold. His hands in particular. His hands were thick, numb, but there was a terrible ache in them, and then he knew he could not stand being here, had to move, had to get out of the water immediately. But where were Ritter and the Indian? The other boat for that matter, with Hudson and Perry, for Godsake? He turned into the fast-falling tide to call for them and was sucking in air to bellow as loudly as he could when the wave lapped up and hit him in the face.

The breath of air he was taking became water. His coughing half emptied his lungs before forcing him to gasp again. But the air that came now was half water, and the burning in his chest wrenched tears from his eyes. The hacking, gagging were uncontrollable, and then he felt himself going down and thrashed out with his arms, kicking, kicking crazily to keep his head up. The panic passed and he was still afloat.

His lungs were mostly clear, rattling slightly, burning. His whole chest burned and ached. The brackish taste and fire were in his mouth and throat. He had to force himself to slow his swimming movements.

Jim Ritter began to sense the Indian's confidence going. With each new course change, he felt his own disorientation increasing. He had reached the point where he was sure they were moving through sections of the same water over again. He hoped he was wrong, hoped the boatman's sense of direction was holding.

The new channel in which they were running bent back up river, away from the village, and Ritter's heart dropped further. But the water had not run out, and now they seemed to be rounding the broad end of a bar that was totally exposed in the low water. Once past it, the channel began coming around, bending toward the open gulf in the direction of the village. Around the bar a heavy gust of wind hit them, but the channel did not shallow out. Then they were running faster, the way opening.

"Good," Michael said loud enough that Ritter heard it over the wind and engine. He saw the boatman wave his arm ahead. They were running directly toward the village, not full speed, but much faster than the slow creeping progress in the labyrinth. Ritter moved into the bow and called Nickerson's name. He called again, and did not stop.

The violent shaking of his body was making the necessary arm and foot movements to stay afloat incredibly difficult for Nickerson. Unpredictable contractions jerked his legs upwards, bent him over in the water, locked him in spasms of uncontrollable shaking.

Then he remembered a survival technique he had read. What you did was grab your air, then let yourself go face down, limp, relaxing as much as was possible, to sink just a little below the surface while you slowly expelled the air in your lungs. Then you kicked up, tilted back your head and breathed again. You were supposed to last like that indefinitely — if the cold did not kill you first.

Nickerson started it. He found with his waders he was sinking so his head would go maybe twelve inches underwater, which was too much, probably, because it was most likely causing him excessive effort to kick back up for air. But the going down and breathing out was sweet, and in a few minutes he was caught in the rhythm of it, almost restful if it weren't for the cold, but even that was lessening. He sank, breathing slowly out, opening his eyes just for a little, seeing the silvery curtain of bubbles that were his breath fleeing up past his face, feeling peaceful in the quiet without the waves.

He kicked frantically, clawing for the surface, breaking through, sucking in the frigid night air. His heart pounded and he gasped not for lack of air, but in terror of how far he had let himself go.

When he was under control, he had to force his body to loosen. He sank again, then rose beautifully perhaps five times, and thought about counting how many times he would do it, unless that would have a sleep-inducing effect like the backwards count from one thousand that your friendly anes-thesiologist calls the countdown into the black hole. No, it had to be good stuff going forward, good to tell them how many times you did it. Figure later how many minutes doing it. Maybe set some kind of record. No records, please. Just hurry up, will you.

He counted up to fifty-two, and on the fifty-third breath he thought his foot hit bottom. He reared back, pawing with one leg like a crazed horse, groping for the solidness he knew was real. It was not bottom, but he was up against something hard, something solid that would not let him go down. He thrashed out with his arms, terrified of dropping to the river bottom, then realized he was moving backwards. Back and up, being lifted . . .

"It's OK. Hold on, I've got you, Ed. It's all right, buddy . . ."

It was Ritter!

Ritter was dragging him into the boat and Ed stopped

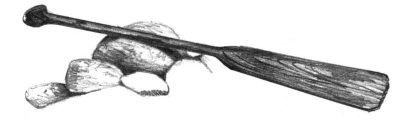

fighting then. They pulled him over the bouncing gunwale, Ritter and the Indian, and he felt himself fall to the bottom of the skiff, sodden, heavy. He was still awake, could hear Ritter talking, saying his name over and over again, asking him to talk, asking if he could.

"Yeah," he managed. "All right, now." It was his voice; he was sure it came from his throat. He tried to sit up, wanted to talk, but they pushed him down on something firm but still giving, and threw something else over him, covering him. There was more noise, then confusion and lights. Flashlights all over, and on him, and he wanted them out of his eyes. He felt the thud of the other boat against theirs, and heard the voices all going at once, Hudson and Perry and the two Indians.

"What in hell happened?" Hudson yelled.

"He tried to walk back," Ritter said.

"Good Lord!" That was Perry.

"It's all right. He's all right, I think," Ritter said. "We just have to get back, get him dry before the wind gets him."

They started the howling engines then, and the skiffs jumped ahead. In a few seconds Nickerson fell from whatever they had put him on, and lay on the hard bottom of the skiff. But that was fine. He slammed when they hit and snapped off a wave crest, and he slid in the grit on the skiff bottom, and that was all right, too. Then he saw the graceful tapered forms two feet from his face. He watched them sliding in unison with him in the grit in the bottom of the boat. They moved forward and back, the rear portions of their bodies in the plastic trash bag. He felt quite friendly toward the two dead salmon.

They motored into a great light, a light that pushed back the night like the floodlights of a ball park. Nickerson struggled up on one elbow and saw they were in the little cove at the village and that the shore was lined with vehicles, their headlights on, high beams shooting across the water. Too much light. It hurt his eyes. He turned back to his salmon, which he could now see shining like pewter in the bottom of the skiff. Their eyes were quite clear, their heads small and beautifully shaped. He put his own head down again. Then they killed the boat engines. The boatmen were out, dragging the skiffs to the beach and there was a lot of talking, soft and controlled.

"They've even got the village police here," Ritter said.

The beach was lined with Indians of the village. Small groups of men and women stood or sat on rocks. Small children played in the sand and ran in the wind.

Hudson, Perry and Ritter were out of the skiffs, wading alongside the boatmen, heading for the beach.

"I guess we're the evening's entertainment?" Perry said.

"Kinda late," one of the village constables said, coming over. "What happened to you guys?"

"Stuck," Hudson told him. "Stuck on the damned bars."

The policeman nodded. "They're bad. Glad you're all right." He looked into Michael's skiff at the two dead salmon and Nickerson lying head to head in the bottom. "What happened to him?"

"Tired," Hudson said. "He's very tired."

In a Place
of Dragons

The old legends say a lake that does not render its dead is a lake in which monsters live. It was one of the nice little bits of lore Roy Angel and the rest of the charter boat captains used to entertain their customers when the fishing was slow. The local monster made good conversation. Tourists liked the idea of there being a sort of water dragon in the lake.

The *real* dragon in these parts came in far more familiar form. Just now he was bellied up to the long bar at the Mooring Saloon, the local watering hole in these parts. The place was crowded this warm spring night in the peak of fishing season, but the high-pitched nasal voice of Vernon Barth pierced the drone of conversation:

"Well, you boys fish today?" he demanded, aiming the

question at the two boat captains to his left, knowing everyone within ear-shot — charter boat skipper or not — would
have been on the water during the past eight hours. He was a
big man in height and bulk, and he tipped a beer bottle back,
downing half its contents after dropping the question. Roy
Angel, drinking nearby with a client, saw the large ring emerald flash on a sausage-fat finger, the hand densely matted
with reddish-blond hair over sun-angered, freckled skin.

The captains grunted a reply, and you could tell they
didn't want the conversation.

"So how'd you do?" Barth persisted. The girl with him
leaned over, caught sight of Angel, and tore her glance away,
her eyes moving nervously, taking in everything, her movements quick, ferretlike. She was slim, maybe too thin you
could say, but exquisitely proportioned just the same, clad in
a pale lilac T-shirt and old jeans that had reached the state
where they would respond to a whisper of contour.

"The fishin' weren't too bad," the nearest skipper answered Barth. "Luke here did a little better than me, I think."

"Lakers?" Barth said. He slid the empty across the bar,
tapped it twice, and brought out a wad of bills with his right
hand. Angel took satisfaction in having got the barman's attention before he could make Barth's refill, but it soured as he
caught the glitter from the big man's other hand as it scattered money. The diamond on the left fist was even larger
than the emerald.

"What are you drinkin', George," Angel asked his client.

"Oh, um, well a gin and tonic, would be wonderful,"
said the out-of-stater. "Remember, I'm paying."

"Nice of you. The usual Rusty," Angel told the bartender. Then added, "Better hurry; Vernon's thirsty." He
cocked his head toward Barth, and the bartender made an
obscene gesture before turning away.

"Yeah, lakers. Couple salmon," the first captain told
Barth.

"How many *you* take?" Barth asked the other skipper.

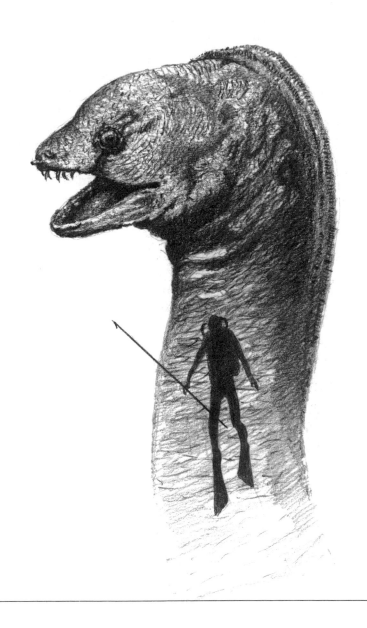

"Oh, hell, one shy of a limit on both," the captain named Luke answered.

"Not bad," Barth said. He tipped the new beer and it bubbled a little around his lips. He put the bottle noisily on the bar. "Took a limit of lakers and salmon," he said. He winked. "Couple more. Released of course." He curled an arm like a stuffed boa constrictor around the girl.

"Did good," said the first captain. Luke said nothing.

That was Barth. You couldn't take away the fact that he caught fish. But he let you know about it — whether you fished just for yourself or were trying to make a living from it. You couldn't take away any of the other stuff he had, either, the lumber business he bought right after he'd slipped into town, then the theater building along with private dwellings, the feed and grain business, the big marina, and just about everything else of value in the area. Oh, and the girl, too. He'd slipped that one to Angel only about five months after moving here. Angel glanced down the bar at Candy. She still looked good, all right. Little Candy Blais. Five months of Barth flashing his rings and paper money, and she moved right in, twenty-five years younger than Vernon, and not caring. Angel turned away quickly, squeezing his glass close to the breaking point, blood pounding in his head. Then he looked up. He stared ahead into the mirror behind the bottles at the back of the bar, his own reflection finally registering — the dark, straight, slicked-back hair, deeply set eyes, face tanned, lean and a little satanic with the nearly pointed ears. Sometimes they called him Old Devil Angel. He felt the rush of anger draining.

"Hey, Roy, didn't see you down there," Barth called, lying, shattering Angel's brooding, yelling over the growing noise in the barroom. "You catch 'em good today?"

Angel shook his head. "Nah," he said.

His client looked at him, amazed. "Why that's not so . . ." he began, protesting.

"Shhh," Angel interrupted theatrically, "We don't need the amateurs tailing us to our good spots.

"Oh," George said.

Barth belly-laughed down the bar, raised his glass.

"Almost no more secret places, Roy," he grinned. "Too dammed many tourists boats out there now."

That there were few secret places left, was true. Before the midday boat traffic had grown, you could keep an eye out for another fisherman getting too nosey about what you were doing, and move off if he started easing in. Now with all the new boaters out there partying, hoping for a look at old Rex, anybody could move in and check you out before you knew it.

Rex was the name of the monster. It was short for Tyrannosaurus Rex, and all wrong, for if there could have been some holdover creature from the Cretaceous Period, it was not going to be a land-bound meat eater. No, it would have to feed on plankton and vegetation. But should it care to consume them, the huge lake offered smelt and alewifes — schools of them that stretched for miles.

"No way to miss you, though, Vernon," Angel yelled down the bar, giving him his shark smile. Barth owned the largest boat around, and it was yellow, bad luck yellow.

Barth nodded, accepting the comment as a compliment even if he might have understood something more in it.

"You're pretty hard to miss yourself," Barth answered. That was true, too. Angel had the only black-hulled boat, but it was the tower that really set him apart, the kind of tower that was standard on offshore saltwater sportfishermen, not a boat fishing freshwater — but then, the lake was nearly like a sea. The added height of the tower gave the same advantage here as it did in the ocean. He could see birds working a long way off, or concentrations of other boats. He could see down in the clear water, too, see color changes and sometimes bottom to help him run contours or currents that fish were using.

"You doin' good enough to make a bet?" Barth asked, knowing Angel was done with that, too, even though the captain had beaten Barth about as many times as he'd lost. The girl, Candy, turned away and stuck her glass out to Rusty for a refill.

"Hasn't been a future in it for either of us, yet," Angel said down the bar.

"I been thinkin'," Barth said. "All these years people talking about it . . . so many people claiming they've seen the thing lately . . ." Barth let it hang, bubbling beer into his mouth. Nobody said anything but you could see the two captains to his left and couples on Candy's side within earshot were all waiting.

"Why is it," Barth continued, "that nobody ever tried to catch old Rex?"

Somebody snorted. Mostly there were grins and glasses raised to drink. Angel shook his head.

"Vernon, a smart businessman like you—you surprise me. Somebody catch old Rex and who'd want to come back to see us?" He saw Candy looking directly at him with a funny expression. He turned back to his drink.

"That's just the thing," Barth said. "We put out the challenge. We put out a price—a big one—for anyone who gets him. You know what that kind of publicity would do? People coming up here to try? How about *that* business?"

"You know the state's got a law against molesting possible lake creatures?"

"But not against studying them—for scientific reasons. So we can't put a price on his head, maybe we make a cash prize for real closeup pictures verified by a couple witnesses. We'll come up with something."

"Who puts up the money?"

"Maybe the town. Maybe the area C of C. Hell, *I* will." He knocked down the rest of his beer and gazed at himself in the mirror behind the bar. "Besides," he said in a little quieter voice but still so everyone close could hear, "I can catch what folks are seeing. I think I can catch the real Rex — photograph him and let him go if I have to, depending on what we find the law says."

Now that he'd gone that far, those close by stopped talking. Then Angel had to speak.

"You're crazy Vernon," he said softly.

"You want to call me on it, Mister?"

"I wouldn't waste my time on that kind of spook chase."

"You don't believe all these people seen *something*?"

"I wouldn't know," Angel said.

"You so sure, how about we make the bet whatever we decide the prize money's gonna be for pictures or whatever in the tourist contest. This season if I don't catch a real, living creature that looks a lot like what folks are describing as Rex, then I eat the cost of the entire prize — which I'm puttin' up in the first place. 'Course if my proof is most believable, then I win the contest anyway."

"That, I'll take you on. Wait, how much prize money you talking about?"

"Well we ought to make it worthwhile to keep folks' interest perked — and bring 'em in. I guess about five grand sounds right."

Angel swallowed hard, realizing it was too late to back out, and nodded. Barth laughed, slapped his big hand down.

"Drinks for the bar," he roared.

And Angel suddenly realized that Barth had worked him into the bet he'd never have taken at first, but the worst of it only hit him now. The word would quickly go out that one of the top charter skippers and a resident recreational fisherman were in a high-stakes race to catch Rex. Which obviously would mean that the charter captain believed in the creature. Which in turn meant Barth had turned him into the ass of the fishing fleet. He gripped his glass, wanting to throw it in Barth's face. When he was able to speak it was in a whispery rasp.

"George," he said to his client, "I gotta go. Right now."

"Are you sure you don't want a refill?"

"No, thanks," Angel told him, standing, pushing away from the bar.

"Hey, you going already?" Barth yelled over. "Listen we'll get together and work out the details and all."

"Right," Angel said, not looking at him, turning away in disgust. He began pushing through the crowd, and suddenly the girl was sliding close to him on her way by. He was rocked by the old familiar scent she used, memories rushing back crazily. He started to speak, but she cut in on him.

"I got to talk with you, Roy," she said quickly. "I'll meet you . . ." Both the time and place were easy — and safe. She turned away, slid through the crowd and was gone.

Alone in the night on his boat in its slip at the old dock, drinking a beer, Angel thought about sea monsters.

He considered the fact that every so many years, presumably extinct lifeforms were found in the oceans of the world. There was the coelacanth, thought gone for 80 million years — since dinosaurs roamed the earth. The coelacanth, with its strange rear dorsal, ventral and pectoral fins on stalk-like appendages, fins used to creep along the 900-foot-deep rocky bottoms where it lived, pursued its prey, consumed it voraciously with needle teeth, spawned its young alive rather than dropping eggs. The first of those creatures taken in modern times came almost fifty years ago off the coast of South Africa, and more of them had followed. Some called coelacanth one of the greatest finds of the 20th century in the quest to learn of life's development on the planet.

Then there was the thing in the Tasman Sea. Commercial Japanese fishermen netted it, hauling the rank, rotted thing from the cool depths, and when they lifted it into the air, swinging the booms close, its decaying stench was so overpowering it was not brought aboard. The remains of the huge creature were unceremoniously dumped; but not before pictures were taken. Not before someone had braved the fetid odor and crept close to cut a specimen from the rotting hulk.

From all those things some believed it to be the remains of plesiosaurus, one of the long-necked, small-headed creatures with paddlelike limbs that swam the oceans during the age of dinosaurs. Even the news magazines had run stories about it.

Angel finished his beer. He checked his watch. And then the situation with Barth flooded back and the hatred rushed through him, finding momentary focus on the empty beer can, which he crushed as though it were paper. He flung it across the cockpit, stood with fists tight against his thighs. He forced himself to stop, then went below. In three more hours he would meet the girl.

The abandoned road cut along a field edge, burrowed into a stand of aspen, then reappeared in a small clearing that faced north, giving a long view of the lake by day. In the darkness a few lights glittered on island camps and along the western lake shore. Angel left his car, walked quietly in low grass toward the cellar hole where a farmhouse once stood. Three fieldstone foundation walls were still intact, banked by earth; the fourth was down. The opening yawned darker than surrounding land contours, like the entrance to some nether world. The girl slipped from the black opening, a floating specter heading directly toward him.

"Thanks for comin'," Candy murmured, moving to him, standing inches from him.

The scent of her perfume assailed him again. So easy now to reach out for her and slip back into the way it had been before.

"What's going on?" he asked her.

"That was it, Roy, the way he set you up like that. I ain't going to be part of that kind of thing no more."

"He's a real sweetheart."

"You don't know half. You don't know what he's doin' to people around here."

"You know how to pick them."

She didn't say anything and he stood there, seeing her shoulders shaking slightly.

"I can't get out," she said finally. "He *knows* about me — all that stuff from before . . ."

"What the hell did you tell him . . ."

"Nothing! He knows."

Angel started to say something, but she cut in.

"I'm going to make it bad for him, Roy. Startin' right now. You got any idea what he's planning on that bet he's got with you? What he's gonna catch?"

"Sure. Money. It's just a gimmick."

"That's only half right. He's gonna catch something and show it. He told me. He's drunk as hell again tonight. He says there's sturgeon — big stuff. And that's what folks are seein'. He found a place. He says they're lake sturgeon, and not coming in from sea but spawning there on ledges because there's no rivers they can go up any more."

"He tell you where?"

"He says he knows for sure."

She explained the place to him, the ledges and the great drop, and he knew the place before she had gone very far.

"Long as I fished this lake I never saw any sturgeon," Angel said. "But I always thought that might be it, if they come up near the top ever and break surface swimming. Now this dude just comes in and finds them — or thinks he has."

"He's been divin'," Candy said.

"What's he planning on?"

"Going to catch one. Said they'd take meat scraps or crawlers in a glob like your fist on a big hook if you laid the bait so it sits on the ledges where they work along suckin' up stuff. He said they're like vacuums with a mouth that comes out like a tube." She shuddered, then continued. "Said if that didn't work he'd spear one."

"Either way it's illegal as hell."

"What would he care? He'll take a picture or make me take a picture, and dump it back. All he has to do is say he caught it by accident. If he has to depend on pictures, he'll wait till he's brought in all the tourist bucks with the contest, then trot out those pictures and claim the money from you. He says them fish are up to maybe eight feet long."

"That's no Rex, is it."

"He says when they swim along the surface they leave a long wake, and people think they're lots bigger."

"If you're not after monsters, those things are plenty big enough. Couple hundred pounds, maybe three hundred at that length."

"If he gets one and a picture, he could convince enough people and win that bet, Roy. You got a spare five grand?"

He laughed sharply.

"You could lose your boat; he could have it held."

"Bet's not a legal contract," he said, knowing that the pressure from the publicly made bet would be almost as binding. "You know when he's going to start fishing for those things?"

"I can let you know. I think in three or four days."

"I guess I'll have to pay Barth a little visit when he's doing something like harassing an endangered species."

"What are you going to do?"

He was silent a moment.

"Depends on how things go. I know what really ought to be done with him. How does any of this help you?"

"Any way I can get at him," she said, "I will."

She leaned slightly closer, tilting her head up toward him in the dark, then placed both hands palm forward on his chest for an instant before turning away.

"I'll let you know," she said, and then she was gone into the night.

The storm began toward dawn. The mid-morning light was as weak as it had been at daybreak. Great ugly clouds the color of bruised flesh tore across a pewter sky. The lake surface was an endless expanse of rollers, running close, breaking and building again, and finally crashing into the sea walls protecting the city. The rain pounded the earth and hurt bare skin. It was a cold spring rain, made colder by the wind. Tourists huddled around the space heaters or small fireplaces in their rental cottages or came to town trying to find something to do.

At the pay phone outside police headquarters, reporter David Flynn was trying to talk to his editor on the large city daily on which he worked. He was a tall young man with bright red hair and pale complexion. He wore a yellow rain suit and low rubber boots.

"Yeah, it's a tourist promo," Flynn yelled into the phone. "No release out on it yet, but they're dropping — get this — five grand on anybody comes up with good shots that prove the thing's real. Nobody says who judges the pix are good enough or prove anything. Yeah, a human interest piece. Lotta locals claim they've seen it. Oh yeah, the guy putting up the money claims *he* can catch the thing. Local fisherman's trying to beat him or something. It's raining like hell; can't do anything else. This doesn't count as vacation time, then, right?" He grinned, rainwater running from his pointed nose.

Flynn hung up, rubbed his hands together, blowing on them for warmth. The rain came hard again. He turned, headed back down the street to the diner where the coterie of regular coffee drinkers who had told him about Barth's pro-

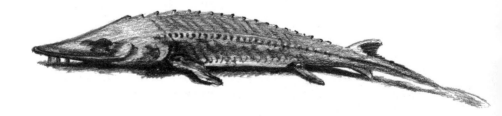

motional brainstorm were holding forth at a corner window table. Should be easy to get some names from them, he thought. Names of residents sure they had seen something. Check the local paper for old stories on the thing. Maybe wrap it all up before the sun starts shining again.

W hy'n hell can't you wait 'til it's done raining?" the girl complained. She carried a load of equipment across the open gas dock at the marina Vernon Barth owned.

"Got to get going, sweetie," he said. "Just dump everything in and get your butt in after it."

He finished pumping gas, jammed the pump hose into the attendant's hands. "Here, let me sign that ticket so your boss won't think you're stealing," he joked. The gas dock was also owned by the marina.

Candy Blais ducked into the cabin out of the rain, looking for a towel. She caught herself from falling as Barth gunned the engine, cut the wheel hard, and headed up the lake into the storm.

They were alone in the driving rain. Neither shore was visible in the gray curtain that surrounded them, and Barth kept well out in the long narrow lake, using his compass to steer, squinting ahead for looming hazards. His navigation skills and sense of place were good. When he slowed the boat and began creeping toward shore, the spot he wanted was perhaps 250 yards distant. He stayed close enough to shore to see it in the rain and pale gray light. The wind had dropped but the rain still fell.

"C'mon out here and steer sweetheart," he yelled suddenly. The girl obeyed, pulling her rain jacket closed.

"Just run this distance from shore," he ordered. "I got the speed set."

He went to the ice chest and took out bulging packages wrapped in waxed butcher's paper. He ducked under the protective overhead, removed a clutter of odd-looking terminal tackle from a locker. He separated sections of newspaper from a short stack of them in the locker, then turned for the packages. He opened them over the rigging table's sink. The girl looked over and was almost sick.

"My *God*, Vernon . . ."

"Pig guts, chicken guts, cow guts," he said. "Got to feed old Rex."

He wrapped double handfuls of the entrails in sections of newspaper, closed the paper, forming little sacks, and wrapped wire around the sack necks. The wire of the sack was attached to a three-way swivel which was also connected to a free-swinging, heavy saltwater pyramid sinker.

"Steer right more," he told her, squinting at some shore mark known only to himself. "Now kick her into neutral."

He clipped a snap at the end of a heavy braided line to the swivel's free eye, waited for the boat to slow, then began lowering the rig. "We're right on," he said. The moment the little bag of animal offal touched the shallow ledge, he jerked hard on the handline, causing the free-swinging sinker to work on the now saturated newspaper. He jerked several more times, knocking the paper sack against the ledge, then quickly brought in the line. The torn newspaper was empty of its repulsive contents.

"There you go," he told her. "Leave a little snack down there for old Rex. Leave a lot of little snacks. All along the shallow ledge. Then we run the next deeper shelves," He grabbed another newspaper sack and motioned her ahead.

"Those sturgeons are gonna have some feast," he said over his shoulder. "Just cruise the shelves with those big old tube mouths extended like a section of empty intestine, suckin' up those nice juicy guts." He smiled imagining the girl's disgust.

"Just what are you going to do?" Candy said.

"Well, catch one, sweetie. I understand it's not permissible to kill one of the things, so we'll just catch one and get his portrait before we put him back."

"Suppose they don't bite?"

"Oh, that's no problem. No, not at all. In that case I just go down and make a call on them, and tickle one of them with this." He went into the cabin and emerged with an underwater spear gun.

She glanced at it, then quickly turned ahead.

"I got a special release head on this shaft," he showed her. "And two T-barbs. See how they curve back when they open? Once that point is in, the shaft breaks free, see. And there's just no way that head will pull out. Just nothing that can get away."

He reached into the cabin, grabbed a vodka bottle from the bulkhead rack, and drank deeply. He looked at the failing day, the rain now stopped, the lake calming.

"Tomorrow we make the contest announcement. Weather's gonna be just swell. We'll do it just after the lake festival kickoff. Maybe get hizzoner up there." He drank again, wiped his lips, grinning. "Gonna make a lot of excitement with that prize announcement. Word'll be out in the city papers by the next day, latest. It's going to be the best season they ever saw here."

"You spear one of those sturgeon things, he's dead, isn't he?"

"Now we wouldn't have to worry about something like that if we never brought him back to dock. But you know 'bout illegal yourself, pretty well, don't you . . ."

She stiffened when he moved behind her. He smiled, walked back into the cabin with the gun and vodka bottle.

"Why don't you kick that throttle into neutral and come on inside a little," he called to her. She did what he asked.

The following morning, Barth added more of the entrail chum. The next day he was on the water before dawn. In the darkness he reached the area of the ledges and the great dropoff. He did not chum. With the girl again behind the wheel, Barth tended his heavy saltwater rods and matching conventional reels. It was tackle never seen, never really needed on the lake, even with the size salmon that were regularly caught, and with the new genetically altered fish that were growing even larger than the first salmon introduced.

The rods were in their gunwale holders, and Barth baited some of the large hooks with pieces of what he had used to chum as the sun heaved up all glowing red and tomato fat. Other rods were rigged with wads of fresh night crawlers pierced through the middles and run up around the hook bend to the eye one after the other until the hook was packed with the writhing creatures. The offering looked like a miniature Medusa. Candy glanced once at the living mass, then quickly turned away.

With the sun low, and Barth now at the wheel, they worked the shallower inshore ledges. There was no wind yet. They inched ahead, stopping from time to time to let the baits sit on a ledge awhile before kicking back into gear. Barth changed the entrail baits every half hour, throwing the water-soaked discards into a plastic pail he kept handy and well covered. The crawlers lasted longer.

At eleven that morning the sun was so hot that it could have been July in Georgia. They had worked all but the deepest ledge before the great dropoff, and now Barth went to his liquor cabinet. He built a tall vodka with tonic, offering the girl one.

They had eaten sandwiches, Barth keeping his glass filled, draining it steadily, then refilling it. She watched him become sloppier in his movements and speech. The ruddiness of his face was intense now, though it could have partly been from heat. They were halfway along the deepest ledge, the boat in neutral, baits on or near the unseen shelf. The lake was oily flat, and although the sun burned unmercifully upon them, a haze was building in the air, taking the sharpness from objects, turning the water gray. Sky over the distant city was smokey, as though industrial stacks billowed their poison into the air, but it was not a factory town.

Barth motioned the girl to move them ahead once more. Exhaust fumes curling up along the transom bent away as the boat rumbled ahead. And then line from one of the stern rods began going out. Barth lumbered for the rod. He slipped off the reel click, thumbed the spool lightly, then pulled the rod from its holder.

"Damn, maybe hung," he muttered. "Hey, stop till I see," he snapped at the girl. She shifted back into neutral.

Barth waited. Nothing happened. He flipped the reel into gear, started to tighten up to free the hook he believed fouled on the ledge when the line went taut and the rod tip bent down. He fumbled again for the lever and snapped the reel back into freespool. The line started out again, slowly, then a little faster, going down.

"God, something big," he breathed.

The girl stood rigidly, back to the wheel, waiting.

The line halted briefly, then started going down again. Barth engaged the reel and struck three times, the heavy mono shooting from the reel in short spurts, slipping the drag. The drag was set heavily, heavier than an experienced blue-water fisherman would have set it, but its only effect was to start whatever was at the end of the line swimming faster.

The big saltwater rod bent and stayed that way. Barth wore no gimballed butt belt, no ocean angler's fighting harness which would have seemed ludicrous here. He jammed the rod below his great belly, feeling the cross cuts of the metal butt end working on his flesh. With the lack of control, something close to fear passed through him like a running shadow. Then he bellowed at the girl.

"For Godsake, get those other lines in!"

Candy uncoiled toward the nearest rod, ripping it from the holder, cranking frantically. The bait came up, dancing on the surface, and she swung it in, letting the foul offering drop to the burning deck. She brought each bait in quickly, each clot of bait slapping wetly on the hot deck. She was nauseated by the stench of the rotting entrails. She opened the airtight pail cover, grabbed the leaders and tossed the baited hooks into the pail.

Struggling to keep his footing, Barth was pulled to the starboard corner of the cockpit. Line still ran from the large-capacity reel. His already flushed face was now an angry red, his breathing loud. He tried to move the rod to a new spot against his body, cutting a line below his stomach with the metal butt.

"Turn us on him!" he called to the girl. "Back toward him!"

Candy ran to the helm, backing as Barth ordered, moving in the direction the line sliced through the surface. They closed quickly, Barth yelling again to stop before they overran the line. For a moment there was the illusion that whatever was hooked had stopped running, and Barth pumped quickly, gaining yardage, glints sparking from the big diamond on his rod hand as it rose and dropped with his pumping movements in the sun. But it was only the slack gained by the backing boat, and Barth's elation died. The line's movement stopped, then reversed direction, peeling effortlessly from the reel.

"Can't put more drag on," he said, voice dry, his breath short.

"What do you want me to do?" Candy yelled at him. She was at the wheel again, hands moving nervously, flitting from the wheel to the controls to the back of the helmsman's chair.

"How the hell should I know!" Barth roared. He looked incredulously at the amount of line gone from the reel. "I can't believe this . . . Just follow if it starts out again."

But it did not. It continued to sound. Barth held on. Finally, he saw it was lost, tightened the drag dangerously, but it made no difference other than increasing the pain from the rod butt jammed against his abdomen. The line did not break. It went nearly straight down off the stern, holding Barth up against the transom, knees jammed there, chaffing, blood pounding in his head in the burning sun.

When the line ran out, the knot held and the rod started down toward the surface. Almost pulled over, Barth reared back with his entire bulk, bending the stiff rod further, reaching up with both hands, up the rod blank. The sound of the breaking line was like a rifle shot. Barth stumbled back, lost balance, and fell heavily to the simmering deck. Candy saw the ugly bleeding cuts below his stomach when his T-shirt pulled away. She started toward him, but he waved her back, rising on his knees, gaining his feet. Panting, sweat pouring from him, he stood bent over, hands on knees, breathing hard for a moment, then straightened, his face contorted by anger. He staggered to the holder that held his half-finished drink, grabbed and downed it. She watched him, saying nothing.

Still breathing hard, he began swearing, then looked at the near shore, lining up marks.

"We hardly moved from the ledge," he said. "It didn't take us any distance — just down."

He turned, stumbled on the rod, groped in a side storage compartment and brought out a marker buoy. He pushed past the girl, took the wheel and headed the boat in the direction he knew the ledge to be. Freeing the lead sinker from the buoy he hurled the marker out.

"Stow that rod," he ordered, his voice hoarse. He went into the cabin. She put up the rod, and when she turned he was dragging his diving equipment from the cabin. He threw mask and fins to the deck, dropped the lead belt, gentled the tank and regulator in the shade beneath the overhead.

"You're not going *down* there," she started.

"Maybe more of them now," he stopped her. "Suckin' up all that good stuff I left for them."

She shuddered. "If that's what it was."

He looked at her quickly, went to the cabin and came back with his neoprene suit and the harpoon gun.

"I got to put this on fast and get in or die of heat stroke," he said. "Gotta wear it or I'll freeze below fifty feet."

"You been drinking, Vernon, you can't dive . . ."

"Shut the hell up." He looked at her with his yellow eyes and she was afraid of him.

She held the tank up as he slipped the weight belt beneath it, spit dryly into his faceplate and leaned backward over the side, crashing to the water. He cleared the mouthpiece, air hissing through the regulator cleanly, slipped the mask over his eyes. He continued to stare at her, reaching up for the gun. He kicked over and descended about thirty feet from the marker buoy.

She turned, frightened, looking around the lake in the building haze, sky darkening to the west, the sun a flat, burning disk overhead. She thought to stop the engine, then worried about being able to start it again if the wind should come as it usually did in the afternoon. She grabbed her head with both hands, staring fixedly at the bubbles coming up like jellyfish where Barth breathed below.

"Oh damn, damn," she said. She looked out at the lake again, and this time to the north, far on the horizon, she saw the dark shape of what seemed to be an approaching boat.

The trail of Barth's expelled air moved to the right, bubbles starting up small, expanding as they reached closer to the surface. They came in bursts from each spent breath.

Candy stood in the pounding sun in the exposed cockpit. She stepped onto the fish box, and now clearly saw the quickly growing form of the approaching boat. It's hull was dark and above its bridge the skeletal frame of the tower was visible. She cupped her hands around her eyes, shielding them, the beginnings of a smile curling the corners of her lips.

When she looked back at the water, fear tore through her.

She could no longer see the bubbles. She scanned the surface, began to panic, then fifteen feet from the boat she saw them. The exhaust of compressed air came as a cloud, not the regulated stream of bubbles, but a sudden burst of wide, silver disks of suddenly released air billowing up to the slick surface, breaking it audibly.

She glanced up quickly, seeing the running boat heeled slightly over, then straightening, skimming fast across the lake in total silence, the sound of its engine not yet reaching her, coming on as though in a dream.

Eight feet off the side of the boat Barth blew through the surface like a breaching whale, shocking her. His left arm thrust high, hand gripping the spear gun. The line tied to it went straight down, and he jerked at the gun, trying to thrust it to her, his diamond ring sparkling on its finger. His eyes fixed on hers in pure horror.

There was a droning sound in her head now as she jumped from the box, a growing drone that did not register as the sound of the approaching boat's engine.

Barth twisted his body, trying to kick closer, trying to reach her outstretched hand to give her the gun, coming up against the taut line like a tethered dog, jerking futilely at the line, the girl's hand just out of reach. Then she saw the line was wrapped around one of his legs. Suddenly he looked down, kicking again, trying to free himself. As though lifted from below, he reared vertically to waist height from the water, eyes rolling in terror, a high-pitched bubbling scream

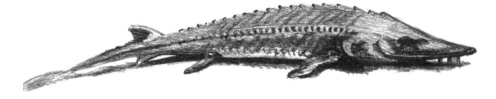

wavering past his mouthpiece, the wail of the mortally stricken. And then he was gone.

"Vernon!" she screamed, her voice echoing his. Then hysterically, "Vernon, Vernon, no, oh, God, no, no, not yet . . ." Then her voice drowned in the thunder of the engine of the black-hulled boat that was upon her.

After working the length of the deepest ledge, the divers came aboard.

"Spook city," the older diver reported. His young partner nodded. "Maybe you can get some of the other guys who're certified to check out the rest of the area."

"What's the matter?" asked the senior trooper.

"Hard to explain," the diver said.

"Those damned eels!" the young diver exploded.

"I don't know what the hell kind of eels you get in a lake," said the older man. "By God they're huge; six, eight feet long, some of 'em. A few are big around as a man's thigh, I'd guess."

The two troopers looked at one another.

"They're laying back up in those caves just under the ledge," the younger diver said. "Couple of them swam past, but mostly they're layin' with their heads and part of their bodies waving out of the caves."

"Yeah, there's a whole bunch of cavern mouths along there. A helluva current coming out of them," the older man reported. "But it's more than that. Funny feeling. Maybe it's the drop. You can see the slope, steep as hell, just going out of sight, and the light angling down. Hard to explain. No sign of him or the girlfriend. Maybe they'll float after awhile."

Captain Roy Angel was working on his boat at the old docks when Flynn, the reporter, found him and went aboard.

"They still going to keep that contest going for anybody who gets pictures of your lake monster?" Flynn asked.

"You'll have to ask the mayor," Angel told him.

"What's your theory — what happened to Barth?" Flynn asked directly.

"Hard to say," Angel told him. "He drank too much."

"And the girl?"

Angel shrugged.

"I understand you and he had a bet — about catching this lake creature."

"That's right."

"What made him think he could catch the thing? What made you?"

"I didn't," Angel said. "He must have."

"Maybe he did. I understand he was a diver."

Angel nodded. "He was a diver."

"How about the girl?"

"Diver? Not that I knew."

"Could he have found something underwater he thought was the thing, and maybe was trying to photograph it and drowned?"

"Who knows? Doesn't explain the girl, does it?" Angel said. "Now that's about all I can tell you. Got to get a few things fixed here. Got a party to take out tomorrow."

"Okay," Flynn said, standing. "Looks like I've got a different kind of story."

He saw that Angel was staring at him.

"It was going to be a fun story — about the contest, about your creature," Flynn said. Then he climbed from the boat, went down the catwalk, and just before reaching the lot where his car was parked, he glanced back. Angel was standing in the cockpit, half turned, as if he were talking to someone in the cabin.

Sharkman

There is a story about the angler who went to Australia intent on fishing for great white sharks. Just before his charter boat sailed, the fisherman suddenly realized what had been bothering him. There appeared to be no bait at all aboard the vessel. The captain was quick to ease concern.

"Don't worry," he told the sport, "it's coming now."

Indeed it was. Being led along the pier in hide that fit like oversize pajamas, plodded an ancient, swaybacked cow . . .

They arrived in darkness. The air was heavy, thick with sea-wet. The two men climbed stiffly from their car after the long drive from the city. They walked with crunching footsteps in the gravel parking lot to the long boat. The boat was the *Huntress*, and she lay clean and white beneath night lights. It was forty-five minutes before they were to sail.

"You want some coffee?" Ed Hammond asked. "There's that diner we just passed. I could use a little walk."

"Sure," the other man said. "Just black."

"Be right back," Hammond said.

Tommy Wakeman watched his friend walk away. He had never seen him stay in one spot more than a few minutes except in a car or on the telephone at his ad agency. Wakeman envied his friend's mountain of energy.

Tommy stretched. His eyes felt gritty from lack of sleep, but otherwise he felt good. He looked forward to the day. Six years of selling magazine advertising space with its ritualistic business lunches was beginning to show around his middle section. Leaning on a strong enough fish or two would be a welcome workout. And kind of a nice way to wind down before the big change came. He thought a moment about Amanda, asleep in her small apartment back in town. They would be married in — he counted — just three days.

When Hammond returned, the two stood sipping coffee gratefully. Boat lights began to wink on slowly, one here, another down the line. There was pale light growing in the east and the stars glittered weakly, fading. The air was rich with the pungent odor of marine organisms living and dead. They scanned the dock for some sign of the Captain. They needn't have worried.

Ten minutes before sailing time the parking lot exploded in a rattle of gravel hurled against wheel wells. Out-of-line headlights caught them as a battered pickup slammed through the lot and skidded to a stop. The engine died, then ran on dieseling before coming to ticking silence. The Captain unfolded from the truck cab looking waxen in the pre-dawn light. Except for his height there would be nothing outstanding about the man to the casual observer. His straight, dark hair was streaked with gray. The hint of fast-growing beard shadowed his jaw. His eyes were what stopped you. They seemed overlarge for the man's angular face, so dark that iris and pupil flowed together, and they were flat, without depth. Perhaps it was just the light. Tommy gulped his remaining coffee.

Walking over, they greeted the Captain with enthusiasm. The man looked at them noncommittedly.

"You boys see my mate yet?" he said when the silence was about to become awkward.

"Don't think so," said Hammond. "He'd be down by the boat, I guess."

The Captain nodded. "Well, you'll see him." He was pulling things from the back of the truck. He looked up smiling with closed lips and Tommy thought he had never seen such a long slit of a mouth. His eyes glittered. "You'll see him if he knows what's good for him," the Captain said.

He turned again, rummaging in the truck, turned and was in front of them suddenly with something swinging in one hand that made them take a quick step backward. In his left hand, held by the ears, were two dead cottontail rabbits.

The Captain headed directly for the boat where a light had just flashed on. As though on cue, a man who must be the mate emerged from the cabin.

"What . . . what are those, uh, rabbits for?" Tommy asked, keeping pace.

The Captain stepped on board. He half turned, mumbling something. It was more the sound of a feeding dog's growl when you've come too near the bowl. Then he ducked into the cabin. Wakeman and Hammond swapped wild glances.

"Morning," the mate greeted them. "How're you fellows this morning?" Compared to the Captain he was a shoulder hugger.

The cabin door opened and slammed. The Captain came out and climbed the ladder to the bridge.

"Name's Guido," the mate told them. "You fellows have everything?"

"Just got to get a couple rods," Ed said.

"Everything's here you'll want," said Guido.

"Well, I'll show you."

Hammond returned with two 30-pound outfits rigged with leadhead jigs. "We'd like to troll out to where you start shark fishing," Ed said. "Maybe later even try sharks with these."

The mate was not enthused. "You might get away with it on the way out. Not sharking." He raised his eyes to the flying bridge. "We do it his way."

"Even if we're paying?" Tommy said.

"Yep. But we catch them when others don't."

Starter motors whirred, straining. The engine caught and rumbled alive. The Captain spread unzipped bridge canvas and leaned out. "Cast off," he told Guido. "We need to kill a shark."

Tommy sat shifting on a bare, side storage compartment watching the day brighten in watercolor blends of palest green, yellow, lilac that blushed into orange-red with the sun's approach.

Guido was cutting butterfish and menhaden into chunks and fillets for bait and chum. The mate worked methodically, slicing and chopping, a chef preparing some magnificent bouillabaisse. Guido kept some of the pieces in containers and scraped some into what was beginning to resemble thick soup. Some of the bait fish were left whole and placed into another container. When he was finished he tied a line to a pail handle, dipped up seawater and began scrubbing down cutting board, deck and transom. When everything was clean he dipped more water, swabbed the deck fresh, cleaned his brushes and mop and racked them. He arranged the chum cans and bait containers close at hand. Then he turned to the tackle.

There was a big 12/0 reel already rigged, but seemingly as a concession Guido went into the cabin and brought back four outfits with 9/0 reels and fifty-pound line. Looking up from rigging his lighter rod, Tommy shook his head.

"You'd think this was Cairns, Australia, or someplace," he said.

Guido smiled faintly, lifting his eyes to the bridge. "A little heavy for blue sharks," he said. "Maybe not for some other stuff that might be there." He began twisting a wire leader to the big snap at the end of the double line on the first fifty-pound outfit.

They headed for the five-mile-wide depression in the ocean floor that was known locally as "the hole." Less than two miles away, the boat slowed slightly and made a small course change. Taking advantage of the reduced speed, Hammond dropped his bucktail over and freespooled it beyond the wake. Tommy was only seconds behind. The leadhead jigs had silver Mylar in the skirts and green plastic teasers on the hooks. They hadn't moved a quarter mile when Tommy's rod bucked once, twice, then held bowed over while line vanished from the reel. He came back unnecessarily hard with the rod, cranked with no effect until the fish slowed. When it did, he lifted and moved the fish. He dropped the rod tip, clamping his thumb on the reel spool, and lifted again. Astern, a bluefish that would weigh well into the teens, thrashed the surface but quickly sounded again. On the other side of the boat Ed was into another.

The boat continued doggedly on course; its momentum, coupled with the anglers' pumping efforts, soon brought the fish on top, slapping then sliding just below the surface toward the boat. Guido gaffed Tommy's fish, dropping it into the fish box, turning, hunting the other blue that had skidded to the starboard corner. The two fish drummed hollowly in the empty box while Guido swabbed the deck. The two men checked their terminal rigs, checked for knicks or frays, sent the now tail-torn lures back again.

"Nice fish," Tommy said. "Big blues."

"I don't mind starting the day this way," Ed answered. The impossible hour at which they had left was forgotten.

In less than a hundred yards travel, the sun bulged over the horizon and both lures were hit hard again, almost simultaneously.

"There must be a big school of them out there," Ed yelled happily. The hooked fish cooperated, tearing off line in separate directions. Suddenly the pressure on both rods lessened though the fish were still there. The boat had slowed, then ceased forward progress altogether. In neutral, the engines rumbled cavernously, changing tone each time the boat wallowed and one exhaust broke the surface.

The Captain was before them. The scimitar-like knife in his hand looked like a slaughterhouse relic. He reached Ed's line first, pulling it down from where it left the tip guide, then slashing the mono with a quick upward thrust.

"What the hell . . ." Ed started.

"We don't want those damned things," the Captain overpowered the protest. His voice was flat and dry. In a quick turn he was on Tommy's line and the man's rod came back straight, a curl of monofilament hanging limply from its tip.

"What's the damned idea?" Tommy began, but again the Captain bulled in.

"You come to fish shark?" he demanded. The wind blew strands of his fine hair wildly like the telltale on a sailboat mast.

"Sure, but . . ."

"Then we fish shark." He pointed at their rods. "Put that toy stuff up. I'm almost there. We got a slick to start." He looked at Guido. "Check that kill stick and rack it behind the bulkhead."

The two men reeled their severed lines back on the spools. Ed shook his head. "The guy's nuts," he said. The boat turned southeast into the steady breeze and soon began to cross the lip of the hole. The rising sun that had shown so much promise slid into a featureless cloud bank and now there was only intense glare and endless grayness in the east. By the time *Huntress* reached the offshore edge of the hole the wind had decreased. The Captain came around, idled checking their drift before he shut down the engines. There was still enough breeze so they would drift generally northwest, crossing the depression, climbing up the far bank.

The Captain leaned out from the controls. "All right," he said.

Guido scooped some of the concentrated mash he had prepared into the larger container that held some seawater and chopped menhaden. Then he stirred and began ladling the swill over. The ocean had gone oily smooth, matching the chum slick which began to coat the surface. There were only occasional heaving swells. With the slick going well, Guido started setting baits. Perhaps as a gesture for the lost bluefish, he set up only the fifty-pound outfits. Instead of the standard long-shank shark hooks there were giant tuna hooks on the leader ends.

The mate cut menhaden fillets, hooking two on a hook.

"A lot of them who fish makos like to hide the hook," he explained. "That's not nearly so important as giving a good size mouthful."

He stripped twenty feet of line from the first reel, wrapped a small plastic foam float to the line with a rubber-band, then sent the baited hook back sixty feet from the boat. The second line was rigged the same way but sct back at forty feet. The third line had no float. It drifted free just thirty feet from the boat.

Gulls screamed overhead, circling the growing slick. Soon the shearwaters moved in across the surface to skim larger bits of fish from the chum. They moved brazenly close to the boat. Guido yelled, waving his arms at them, but it did no good. Up in the bridge the Captain had removed the canvas doors and side curtains. He sat watching, a form without features in thc shadow below the bridge overhead. No one spoke. In the silence, at wide-spaced intervals, a swell would come large enough to break past the boat with a hissing sound. And there were the cries of birds. Nothing else. Suddenly, the click on the port-side reel rattled a short, staccato burst, jolting Wakeman and Hammond from torpor, onto their feet, hearts pounding. Guido was already at the rod, cursing. One of the shearwaters had hit the line, caught in it briefly. The Captain had not moved.

The day turned grayer still except for the sky directly overhead, which looked as though it were polished by a rarefied wind. Around them, though, the breeze remained gentle and the day grew hotter. The breeze squirreled occasionally into the east with little puffs that curled the stench of putrefying chum from the containers around in the cockpit. Guido kept the slick going. Occasional spatterings of the liquid hit the transom or gunwales, turning brown as they dried. The boat wallowed in the valleys of the swells drifting slowly, and dullness settled in, deadening senses. As they neared the inside slope of the hole the bottom began its long, gentle climb to two hundred feet.

A quarter mile away and sixty feet beneath the ocean surface, one, then two beautifully sleek cobalt shapes turned to cut the drifting chum trail. From below, their undersides were the dead white of something that has never seen the sun. They were male blue sharks, and as they crossed the trail of chum again, their excitement grew, visible in quickening tail beats and body thrusts. A third shark joined them, and as a loose group they rose higher, gliding forward, hunting the source of the rich slick which signaled something helpless on which to feed.

More large pieces of fish flesh were suspended in the water the closer the sharks came to the boat, and the blues took them with quick snapping movements, rising, rising, until 150 feet from *Huntress* their fins cut the surface.

There was a thud of feet on the bridge deck. Tommy and Ed turned to see the Captain standing, his long-muscled arm pointing out straight. His mouth stretched in a wolfish grin. "They've come, boys," he said without looking down. "There they are." It was the closest they had seen him express something that resembled happiness.

Guido scattered two more ladlefuls of chum, slammed several butterfish overboard, then took two rod belt harnesses from their hooks.

"Unless we're into something really big we don't use the chair," he told the anglers. "Give you more fun with those blue sharks standing up."

From the bridge burst a rumble of deep laughter that bordered on the demonic. Ed and Tommy looked up but could see nothing. Guido continued to watch the sharks. Smiling his great slit-mouthed smile the Captain went to a mahogany cabinet. He removed a bottle of blended rye whisky from its shelf, cracked open the screw top, and took two long, gurgling pulls. "So they came again," he muttered, as though it were a personal triumph. "They never get enough." He returned the bottle to the locker. A drop of amber distillate glistened in the beard stubble near one corner of his mouth. He wiped it with the back of a sun-pocked calloused hand, without brushing away the smile.

"They're here all right, boys," he boomed down. "Now get yourselves ready." Once again the deep laughter thundered at them.

Hammond rolled his eyes. Tommy just shook his head, watching the closing fins.

The blue sharks reached the middle bait, snapping small morsels of flesh.

"Lead fish is a *damned* big blue," Guido said. "He'll go nine feet, anyway."

As he spoke, the fish sounded and the cork on the middle line popped free. Immediately, the reel click went off like an old-time New Year's Eve noisemaker. As Guido lifted the rod to Hammond, who was closest to him, the fish came up again, moved to the float of the near line, and confidently ate it. Yelling, Guido yanked the line which somehow popped free. "Get that line in and check if it's frayed," he yelled at Tommy.

Ed snapped off the click, jammed the rod butt into his fighting belt and used his thumb to control the line that was running steadily out.

"Hit him now!" Guido ordered.

Ed slapped the lever over and came back hard twice. The

rod bent and stayed that way. Line skidded from the reel, against the drag.

Another burst of laughter rippled from the bridge.

"Watch that far line now," Guido told Tommy. "You see him take that float? They do that sometimes. They take the farthest bait, then come in and eat the other baits or floats before you know it. They don't even know they've swallowed hooks," he said. "That line all right?"

"It looked fine," Tommy said.

"Now watch that far line," Guido repeated. "If his fish doesn't get in the way you may get tight."

The blue shark made two dogged runs out and down and Ed pumped it back nicely. Now it was closer to the boat, trying to beat straight down. The float on the outboard line began moving off. It had not popped but was skidding across the surface.

"There you go," Guido warned.

Tommy had the rod, and when he struck the float came free.

It was a smaller shark than Ed's but it ran strongly against the drag and Tommy let it go, enjoying the power of the run before trying to turn the fish. The first blue was at boatside now, spinning wildly. Guido grabbed the leader with gloved hands. Water exploded into his face.

"This is a good blue; you want him?" The mate yelled. The shark thrashed against the side. "We cut them off unless they're this big or you want the jaws."

"No, let him off," Ed said.

Guido ran his pliers down the wire, cutting as close as possible to the shark's head. The wire parted instantly and the shark rolled over once before gliding out of sight.

"Blues eat rotten anyway," Guido said. "We should get something else if you want to keep teeth. Maybe dusky. Mako, if we're lucky. Don't count on whites. We'll keep any mako."

Tommy had worked his fish in now, and Guido took the leader.

"Cut it off," Tommy said. "I'll gamble for something bigger."

Again, the Captain was behind them, having appeared almost magically.

"First blood, boys," he said happily. "It's going to be a good day." He ducked into the cabin, reappearing with another rod and reel. "Another bait," he told them. "If they all go off together you'll have to dance."

Guido was already sending out fresh baits, keeping the chum going with his other hand. The Captain placed the bait on the new rod just slightly inside of Guido's sixty-foot float. There were four rigs set now, three with foam floats bobbing nicely. The sharks came again.

The first blue sharks, including the ones they released, had circled out, but there were others closer to the boat, sliding just below the surface, rolling easily. A grayer form with blunter snout appeared briefly near the float of the second line out.

"Dusky there," the Captain pointed. "We're on a roll boys. Get them now before it dries up."

Before he could speak again, the float where the dusky had been, disappeared. The Captain plucked the rod from its holder, swinging to Ed nearest to him, thrusting the rig into his belt and hands with such force, that Hammond felt as though he were impaled. When he set the hook the fish went down like lead. This was nothing like the fight of the blue shark. Ed spread his feet, tried to brace himself, tried to lean back but stumbled forward.

"Pull," boomed the Captain. "Break your backs, boys." He was not looking at them but watching the floats and the shark fins cutting the surface. "Pull your guts out boys, it's what you're paying for."

"More blues out there," Guido said. As though in response, the farthest float began to move off at the same moment the closest rig disappeared. Tommy saw Guido had the far rig, and took up the near rod. Before he could do anything the Captain's voice hit him.

"Feed line," he ordered Tommy. "Don't put pressure on." He grabbed the rod he himself had rigged. "Damned blues, now," he rumbled. He pulled the float, trying to take the bait away from a blue shark near it, but was too late. The rod bucked. There were four fish on now, and bedlam reigned. The Captain responded like an overwound spring, suddenly released. He screwed down the drag dangerously, came back on the blue so hard with a series of lightning fast jolts that the fish must have been pulled up and over like a chained maddened dog hitting the end of its tether. The small shark never had a chance. It was pulled in like some planing board, first on the surface, then just below. The Captain countered every sideways thrust it attempted, forced around its head, totally dominated the creature.

"I'm off," Guido yelled. His fish had broken free and the mate cranked his hookless line in wildly. "Your fish still there?" he asked Tommy.

"I think . . . yes, there goes the line a little again."

Over in the port corner where the fish had brought him, Ed strained against the dusky, trying to bring the rod up to get line, watching what little he gained slip out again.

Teeth clamped, his face void of expression, the Captain bulled his shark in mercilessly, dropped his rod, held the leader with one hand, clipped the wire, then ran the rod and reel back out of the way near the cabin bulkhead. There was a bump then a thunking vibration from below decks. "They're on the props," he said.

Tommy looked at him wide-eyed.

"They'll try to eat anything in the water, now" the Captain said.

To prove him right, two blue sharks emerged from beneath the boat and ran its length. One of them rolled, looking up for a moment, its cat-like eye just below the surface. Then it disappeared.

The Captain turned on Tommy. "Take that slack up, see where he is and hit that fish."

On the free line, Wakeman's shark had never gone from the chum slick. It was still on the opposite side of the boat from the dusky. Tommy took slack line in quickly, tightening up, then knocking the reel into gear. He hit the fish. It was maybe thirty feet from the boat.

In actual time, it took just seconds, but to Wakeman it was like a slow-motion film. The ocean surface blew apart in a perfect, foam-fringed circle and something pale colored, something very big, rose into the air and seemed to hang there at the apex of its leap before turning over backwards, almost lazily, in a nearly complete flip. The creature crashed heavily back, slamming the surface like a concrete slab pushed off a three-story building.

The line burned from his reel with a dry, buzzing sound. He heard the Captain's voice crack one word. "Mako!" Tommy felt his line stop, sag briefly. He cranked furiously, then saw the clear nylon begin angling to the left. And then the big mako came up again. The fish boomed into the air in one head-over-tail leap, crashed back in, then exploded a second time into the sky. Again, it came up on a totally reversed course. It happened so quickly the huge boils from each leap were still visible on the ocean's surface before the shark crashed down the third time.

The mako veered to port where Hammond was still fast to the dusky, now farther from the boat. Ed felt the shadow of something over him, turned and saw the Captain. He saw the brightness of steel in the gray light, the quick movement as though a dark bird's wing had passed over head. And then the pressure on his rod was gone. He looked up, pained.

"I want that mako," was all the Captain said.

Ed stumbled shakily toward the cabin, laid his rod against the bulkhead. He felt weak. Now it was Tommy's turn. The mako was on another tack, giving the angler a chance to gain line. It lasted only a moment. Again the fish ran and Wakeman, on his feet, was dragged in a crab shuffle toward the opposite side of the boat. He came up against the unpadded wood gunwale, slamming his knees painfully, trying not to bend over.

"You lose that outfit and you're in after it," the Captain warned.

Long minutes passed in strained standoff.

"Stop resting him," the Captain said.

Tommy managed to raise the rod and move the fish. He dropped the tip, then repeated the action, mechanically. The mako came a little way then burned off again, taking all the gained line plus a little more. But there was no jump. Thirty minutes later Guido guided Wakeman to the chair. The relief to his legs was a gift. No longer was he forced to fight to keep erect against the mako's direction changes. The pale blue jeans he wore were blotted dark from blood around the knees where he hit the gunwales, but he felt no pain. What hurt were his arms, shoulders and back. Especially his forearms. His mouth was drier then he ever remembered. Guido poured some water and held the cup for him to drink.

An hour later he was ready to do almost anything to end it and hide somewhere in darkness. Forty minutes more and the mako was coming in. It made small lunges now, then heaved halfway from the water in a final effort to leap. Tommy was beyond summoning a final surge of energy. He cranked and pumped raggedly like some antiquated machine.

Close to the boat, the fish went down, but just a little way. Tommy raised him.

"Get up," ordered the Captain. "Move him along the side, and bring him in. Back yourself."

Tommy obeyed, stumbling, not trusting his legs. Guido had the leader, held, lifted. The Captain reached with the flying gaff, sank the plow-pointed head deeply, and the shark went wild, spinning in a concussion of foam and water. The leader snapped. The line from the gaff head was tied to a bit on the boat, and when the fish quieted a little, the Captain pulled it close again. Guido used a straight one-piece gaff to bring the tail up. The Captain dropped a loop of heavy line over it and came tight. They held the shark shuddering there.

"It'll go close to four hundred," Guido said. The Captain went to the controls. He started the engines, threw over an unanchored marker buoy, then began moving ahead in a slow forward arc that took him away from the chum slick.

Hammond had taken the rod from his friend. Tommy sat dazed. Sweat matted his hair. His shirt clung to him. His face was slack. Hammond gave him water. When he was finished he handed Tommy a beer.

"I can hardly hold it," Wakeman said.

"You did all right," Guido told him. He clapped Tommy's shoulder and the angler thought he'd fall over. Ed was talking when they both realized the boat had made a huge circle and was now headed back toward the marker. And the slick. From the primary controls the Captain turned. His eyes were bright and he was smiling, all teeth showing.

"We've got them coming boys," he said, his voice rich and full. "Now we have a mako. God knows what else will come."

No more, Tommy thought. I won't touch a rod. I can't handle anything more. Let Ed do it.

When they were back in the slick the Captain helped Guido lash the shark fore and aft alongside.

"We'll bring him in when something tries to eat him," said the Captain. "He's dead, but they don't stay that way much."

Guido started the chum again. Tommy looked over the side at the big mako, a nosegay of uneven teeth blossoming from its mouth, the flat dark eyes looking as though they had never been able to see.

Two more blue sharks came later. They made Tommy take a rod, and when he broke off, he silently thanked whatever fates were responsible. Later that afternoon, another dusky ate the twin fillet of menhaden and Ed worked him frantically, but this time there were no knives. When it became apparent that the fish was tiring the Captain sprang from his bridge aerie. He put Guido on the mako's tail rope. He took the forward line himself, and together they worked the carcass into the boat. It fell in, stiff and heavy, puddling gore, and Tommy moved quickly away. They raised the mako's tail section toward the superstructure to rest against the spar that served as a gin pole. The shark was then secured forward and aft. Then they turned to Hammond.

Along with fear of losing the fish, Ed sensed the lateness of the hour. He strained against the shark, anxiety whining in his head. But the dusky was coming. When it was over, the shark alongside, the Captain shouted before Ed could open his mouth.

"Gaff him," the Captain ordered Guido. "Don't turn him loose." He ducked into the cabin while the mate sank the clean stainless gaff hook. The shark's thrashing hammered the gaff handle violently, forcing Guido to fight for balance.

The Captain returned with the killstick. He dropped a charge in the powerhead, screwed it closed, and waved Hammond back. He went to the side, came over, two-handed, brought the 12-gauge head down surely. There was a thudding report. The shark shuddered violently, then was still. He had Guido raise the dusky halfway from the water, still keeping the shark over the side while he watched it.

Ed leaned against the far side. Finally satisfied, the Captain and Guido brought the dusky over. It was a good fish, slightly lighter than Tommy's mako. The mate began hoisting the fish up, beside the mako.

"Wait," the Captain told him. He returned to the cabin, and when he reappeared he carried a long wood swab handle. In his other hand he carried the two dead cottontail rabbits. They looked stiff and flat and totally out of place.

"Drop that snout," the Captain ordered. Guido lowered the shark's tail and went to its head. The Captain placed the rabbits almost tenderly in shadow on the deck. He grasped the wood handle in two hands and began working at the shark's mouth. The end of the handle burred and splintered. He dropped it in disgust, went back to the cabin rack and returned with a harpoon shaft. With Guido's help he finally spread the jaws as far as possible. He took the first rabbit and thrust it into the dusky's maw. He took the burred wood handle, pounded the cottontail deeply down the shark's gullet.

Tommy and Ed watched, incredulously. The mate, who had learned to accept each new turn of the Captain's virtuosity, contained himself with effort. Now the second rabbit followed the first. The Captain plunged and pounded. Guido

straddled the shark, straining at its snout. Gulls screamed. Lost in his world, the Captain worked feverishly, chortling, mumbling to himself. His hair flew like Maypole streamers. When it was done, he straightened.

"String him up," he told Guido.

The Captain's eyes slid like a lizard's over to Ed then back to Tommy. He mumbled something as he turned, then started laughing as he climbed to the bridge. It was not a totally unpleasant laugh. The two friends sat in disbelieving silence all the way back.

The precise moment that *Huntress* rounded into the harbor, the bank of grayness in the sky parted. The sun was orange-golden, sinking quickly, growing fatter, shimmering as it did. Above the dock, the evening crowd was waiting for the returning boats. There were children, mouths rimmed in residual ice-cream crust; the svelte, the bulbous, the old and the prime. As the boat turned prettily toward her slip, they pushed forward excitedly, murmuring. Some pointed.

The boat pulled neatly in, reversed engines, stopped dead. Guido was out quickly making lines fast. Then the unloading started.

The sharks were slid from the boat and winched high beneath the charter boat's sign across the entrance to the slip. The crowd grew louder as the huge fish inched to their final triumph. Tommy and Ed collected their gear. They paid the Captain.

"You'll want the mako," he informed Tommy. "Guido will steak him for you; ask him. The jaws are yours, unless you don't want them."

The fishermen agreed. They didn't know what else to do.

Then it began. The Captain strode from his boat. The late sun glinted from the large knife in his hand. He ignored the spectators, going directly to the sharks. He pulled up on the snout of the mako revealing the awesome rows of violent-looking teeth. The crowd murmured again; fearful sounds. Children were lifted to shoulders to stare with eyes like small raisins in faces of whole-grain pudding. Some of them turned away.

The Captain went to work carefully on the mako's jaws. It was a bloody job, but soon he had freed the hinged cartilage. He set the jaws aside in a large pail, straightened, and for the first time acknowledged the spectators while wiping his knife.

"How'd you like to pay the dentist bill for one of these beauties," he said. There was a weak titter of laughter. "Let's see what these fellows have been eating," he added.

Guido began trimming flesh from the mako's jaws. The Captain turned his knife to the thick dusky. The skin was tough but he worked through it, spreading and emptying the shark. A few of the spectators left. More refused to look — momentarily. Most of them pressed forward, and now one, then another pointed. Voices grew louder. There were a few unbelieving gasps. A child began to cry. The stiff forms of the wretched cottontail rabbits had been revealed. The crowd grew noisier. For one woman it was too much.

She was short, blocky without being fat, and her hair resembled a used SOS pad. She clumped down to the dock in a nimbus of indignity. She jounced right up to the Captain, looked down at the rabbits, then thrust her chin at the man towering above her. She gathered herself, took a deep breath and in a voice that had ordered countless bowls of chicken soup for a generation of children and grandchildren, she spoke.

"Can you explain," she demanded, "how two land animals happened to be inside this . . . this fish?"

The Captain had played it perfectly, and now he approached Shakespearean eloquence. He looked once at the crowd, then at the woman. He swelled, readied himself.

"Madam," he said, "this is one of the mysteries of the deep we'll never understand."

The woman's mouth dropped. The crowd stilled for a moment before returning to its babble. The Captain strode from the dock and up to the parking lot. Crossing the distance to his truck he began humming little bits of something that sounded, if you listened closely, very much like a verse from the *Battle Hymn of the Republic*. In his truck he slammed the door, opened a window. Now he was singing the words in a gentle rumble to himself. He reached into a small beverage cooler, plucked out an icy beer and started off, still singing. He sang aloud, inspired, "His truth is marching on!" He drained half the beer, belched once, contentedly, wrapped himself around the steering wheel and rattled off into the gathering dusk.